ANCIENT THOUGHTS IN MODERN PERSPECTIVE:
A CONTEMPORARY VIEW OF THE BIBLE

Ancient Thoughts in Modern Perspective: A Contemporary View of the Bible

SOLOMON POLL

PHILOSOPHICAL LIBRARY

New York

PRINTED IN THE UNITED STATES OF AMERICA

Foreword

Every generation, it is said, must re-write history for itself. The past says different things to different people and the richness of the lessons to be gleaned from what has happened long ago is very much a function of what the viewer brings to bear in his search. The Bible is, of course, far more than history. It is a store-house of learning and precept; it invites exploration. The richer the background of whoever would fathom its contents, the sharper his insight, the richer the treasures it will yield.

Professor Poll's contribution in this book is a reflection of the great erudition which he brings to bear as he studies the ancient texts and their modern implications. He is at home in medieval rabbinic literature, thoroughly conversant with the exegetes, both ancient and modern, and, it should occasion no surprise, he is a master of contemporary scholarship in sociology, his chosen field.

As one pages through this volume, the range of references and the range of interest are striking: aesthetics, psychology, group theory, theology, race relations and ethics. Skilfully interwoven with text and commentary, all these, and more, add to the brilliance of the resultant tapestry.

Dr. Poll, clearly enough, speaks in the modern idiom without diluting the authenticity of the ancient verities. His erudition does not intrude. Indeed, this book had its genesis in a series of columns which soon became one of the more popular features of the Philadelphia *Jewish Exponent*. Writing weekly in a journal of wide circulation, Dr. Poll attracted thousands of regular readers. They were of varied backgrounds and differing tastes, but united in interest in at least one respect, in the desire to understand better the contemporary implications of their Biblical heritage.

Our generation has need of lessons from the Bible, lessons which are at once relevant and intelligible. We are challenged to reaffirm or to reject moral values in many spheres, from national policy to personal relations. To do either, and to be able to explain what we

vii

have done, requires understanding. We have need of the experience of search and research in the treasure-house of tradition, creative search, but one true to the letter and the spirit of the texts it expounds.

Dr. Poll's writing helps meet these needs. He offers the stimulation of challenge and the challenge of stimulation, and with it all the promise of a deeper, more satisfying understanding of a vital heritage.

A. Leo Levin

TABLE OF CONTENTS

TABLE OF CONTENTS—*Continued*

Author's Preface

Throughout the ages the Jew had considered his existence eternal, immortal, and forever dynamic. Even Moses when he addressed the children of Israel before he died said, "this covenant is made not with you alone but both with those that are standing here with us this day . . . and those who are not with us here this day." Ever since that declaration, the Jew had committed himself and the generations that followed to carry on his tradition. In every country, in every city and in every hamlet into which the Jew was dispersed he confirmed again and again that his Jewish life with all its meanings and complexities, with all its pains and pleasures he would further and cultivate. He pledged to sustain, to persist, and to preserve this form of life that had given meaning to his existence through so many generations.

This very life, this unshakeable trust was threatened by the systematic physical destruction of the Jews in Europe. In moments of agony, of despair and dissolution, when my parents together with millions of Jews with no resistance but their passionate knowledge of their Jewishness, were taken to concentration camps—I too thought that this Jewish life, that these generations of tradition would disappear mingled with the smoke of their destruction.

Through innumerable miraculous events some of us survived and tried to transmit to future generations the one thing that remained from the past, the zealous determination to continue this Jewish life. Thus, even today the old covenant, the ancient thoughts in modern perspective are not with us alone but with those that have passed and those that will follow.

These sentiments were the main reasons that moved me to accept an invitation from the *Jewish Exponent* to write weekly essays on the Torah. These essays were published in a series in the *Jewish Exponent* in the years 1963-1964. I anticipated that upon their completion I would have them published in book form. The essays are independent of each other, however, they try to express a modern perspective based upon an ancient thought.

In connection with this work I express my thanks to Mr. Sylvan B. Kling, former editor, and Mr. Charles S. Shapiro, editor of the *Jewish Exponent*, for their cooperation and help. To Professor A. Leo Levin, Vice-Provost, University of Pennsylvania, who was President of the *Jewish Exponent* at the time the articles were first published, goes my deep appreciation for his continuous encouragement, for his editorial criticisms and comments. To my wife goes my deep affection for her patience and strength.

I wish to acknowledge the generous financial support of the Central University Research Fund of the University of New Hampshire that made the publication of this book possible.

SOLOMON POLL

I. From
THE BOOK OF GENESIS

1. "In the Beginning God Created ..."

"In the beginning . . ." were the opening words of the first book of the Bible. In Hebrew the book is called *Beresheet*, literally, "in the beginning," after the first word of the verse. In English it is called *Genesis*, meaning "beginning" or "origin," which title comes through the Vulgate from the Septuagint.

The text reads, "In the beginning God created heaven and the earth. And the earth was unformed and void, and darkness was upon the face of the deep . . . And God said 'let there be light' and there was light. And God saw the light that it was good; and God divided the light from the darkness . . ." (*Genesis* 1:1-4)

The interpretation of the first verses of the Torah gives much difficulty to the traditional, as well as to the modern, scholars of the Bible. For example,

a) The term "in the beginning" cannot mean "first," because the heaven and the earth were not created first.

b) If light was created on the first day, what did it consist of? It could not be the sun, because the heavenly bodies were created on the fourth day.

c) From the text it seems that there was water before the heaven and earth were created; thus, when did God create the water?

d) If the term "heaven and earth" is an inclusive term, suggesting that all else was created with the creation of heaven and earth, then, what is the real order of creation? (*Malbim*)

Despite the difficulty the first verses present in the understanding of the sequence of creation, nonetheless, for the Jew the opening verses manifest the basis for his theological system. "In the beginning God created . . ." conveys to the Jew the basic fundamentals for his unusual faith in God. It signifies the unconditional creatorship of God.

To the Jew the "universe did not come into existence by chance. It did not advance by blind gropings of unconscious energies. It was not some dark welter of lifelessness inexplicably evolving into life.

3

On the contrary, it was the purposeful creation of Him who is the fount of life . . . " (*The Interpreter's Bible*, Vol. 1; p. 467)

The creation of the heaven and the earth indicates a specific dichotomy in the arrangement of the world. The universe, as well as the universal comprehensiveness of the affairs and interests of humanity, are divided into *heaven,* or the heavenly, and *earth,* or the earthly.

The whole range of life's activities fall within the scope of *sacred* and *profane. Sacred* encompasses all that is holy and *profane* all that is secular.

Religion conceives man to be composed of body and soul. The body, being the organism or the physical substance, is manifested in man's external behavior, and the soul, being the spiritual substance, is manifested in his moral emotional nature.

These divisions are not only prevalent in the field of religion. Modern social and behavioral scientists also utilize this sacred-secular dichotomy. Psychologists speak of an *id* and a *super-ego. Id* represents the rash, uncouth, animal instinct of man, whereas the *super-ego* represents the trained, the educated, the socialized man who knows better.

Furthermore, references are made to the external man and his unsophisticated, raw physical strength on one hand, and the internal man with a conscience, full of moral and ethical values, on the other.

Sociologists speak of *primary* and *secondary* group relationships. Primary groups are those in which the individual himself counts as a whole person, where the relationship is based upon love and personal intimacy.

Secondary groups are those in which the individual himself does not count as a person, he can be replaced by others; he is only a number or a statistic, without any personal significance.

The question is asked, again and again, what is predominant in man, the *sacred* or the *profane?* Which part of him subordinates the other, the id or the super-ego, the external man or his conscience? What type of relationship is man seeking, primary or secondary groups, in order to maximize his potentialities?

The Midrash relates that Bet Shamai and Bet Hillel were debating the question, what was created first, the heaven or the earth. The School of Shamai maintained that the heaven was created first, as it compares to a king who first made his throne and then his footstool. Thus, according to this view, the heavenly is predominant and

4

the earthly secondary. It is the heavenly upon which the earthly can be built.

The School of Hillel maintained that the earth was created first, as it compares to a king who built a palace in such order that first he constructed the lower part and afterwards the upper part. According to this view, the earthly is predominant upon which the heavenly can be built.

Rabbi Simeon, however, observed, "I am amazed that the fathers engage in this controversy, for surely the heaven and the earth were created simultaneously, like a pot and its lid." (*Midrash Rabbah Genesis* 1:15)

Both components are equally necessary! The sacred, the heavenly, as well as the profane, the earthly must be utilized in the same degree in order to function effectively. It is necessary to use godliness in the performance of the earthly, and it is equally necessary to utilize the earthly in matters of the godly. The transmission of one to the other is, however, the great challenge for man.

2. Coexistence or a Tower of Babel?

The story is told of how man attempted, in order to make a name for himself, to build a tower with its top in heaven. The text reads, "All the earth had one language and the same words. And as man migrated from the East, they came upon a valley in the land of Shinar and settled there. They said one to another . . . 'Come let us build us a city, and a tower, with its top in heaven to make a name for ourselves; else we shall be scattered all over the world!'

"And the Lord came down to look at the city and the tower which man had built, and the Lord said, 'If, as one people with one language for all, this is how they have begun to act, then nothing that they may propose to do will be out of their reach. Come, let us go down, and there confound their speech so that they shall not understand one another's speech.'

"Thus the Lord scattered them from there over the face of the whole earth, and they stopped building the city. That is why it was called Babel, because there the Lord confounded the speech of the whole earth, and from there the Lord scattered them over the face of the whole earth." (*Genesis* 11:1-9)

5

It is interesting to observe these passages as they symbolically reveal man's great compulsion and aggression throughout the generations. In every era man wanted to build a tower reaching to heaven. He was building devices and technological instruments. He designed, contrived, and schemed to reach higher and higher than his capabilities.

Man was always hostile about his physical and mental limitations and restrictions. He always rebelled about his confines and boundaries. Man was always envious of the infinity, the boundlessness and the eternity of God. So he always reached far beyond his capacities. And, as he was unwilling to recognize his limitations, he became ostentatious, pretentious and arrogant.

Egyptian Pharaohs wanted to perpetuate their fame and themselves with obelisks on which they engraved the record of their honor and accomplishments. Each monarch built his own pyramid, in which he tried to preserve his mummified body for eternity. The construction of these pyramids took years and measureless amounts of material and human labor. (*Interpreter's Bible*, Vol. 1, pp. 562-565)

The great pyramid of Khufu or Cheops (reigned c. 2900? B.C.) at Giza near Cairo, for example, is a solid mass of limestone block, covering 13 acres. It was originally 768 feet square, and 482 feet high. This pyramid is still standing today, but only to symbolize a civilization that drifted near decay.

Greece glorified in its architecture, in its Doric, Ionic and Corinthian styles exemplified by the Parthenon on the Acropolis at Athens (447-432 B.C.), Temple of Athena Nike at Athens (c. 426 B.C.), and the Olympeum at Athens (174 B.C. - A.D. 131). But "the glory that was Greece" is hardly a memory today.

Civilizations such as Babylonia, Assyria, Persia and Rome all tried to build up empires through strength and power and wanted to assume the tower of authority "with its top in heaven." Today their claim is only to posthumous fame.

The modern world is also building its tower of Babel. With the immense industrial resources, with the scientific inventiveness, with the economic mastery, with the control of atomic energy, with the possession of ballistic missiles, with the stock-piling of hydrogen bombs, with the competition of rocketry into space, the tower is being built higher and higher, with its top in heaven.

And now the call goes out, ". . . let us move the steep and difficult path . . . through mutual verification . . . There is room for new cooperation, for further joint efforts in the . . . exploration of space . . . and a joint expedition to the moon. Space offers no problem of sovereignty . . . Why . . . should man's first flight to the moon be a matter of national competition?

"Why should the United States and the Soviet Union, in preparing for such expeditions become involved in immense duplication of research, construction and expenditure?

"Surely . . . the scientists and astronauts of our two countries— indeed of all the world—should work together in the conquest of space . . . not as the representatives of a single nation, but as representatives of all humanity." (President John F. Kennedy's address to the United Nations, Sept. 20, 1963).

Is it not ironic that we are advocating that American and Russian explorers arrive hand in hand to the moon, while there is much dissension here on earth? Is it not ironic that the cooperation and unification of all humanity is called upon for the purpose of building a new tower of Babel, reaching heavenward, to the moon today, and tomorrow with its top in heaven?

Thus, the whole earth has one language; there is practically an agreement among the nations as the cry goes out "Come, let us build a tower with its top in heaven!"

But the Lord came down to look at the tower which man had built, and He said, "As one people, with one language for all, is this how they have begun to act . . .?" If unanimity among men is only for the purpose of building another tower of Babel, *"Come, let us go down,* we cannot wait until all human beings are exterminated, but rather make a separation among them with their languages." (*Malbim,* Vol. 1, p. 29)

At this point, God confused their language, suggesting that there is no unanimity, but a spiritual confusion that is afflicting man. Men talk at cross purposes thereby alienating one from another.

There is a depravity in man's deep and inner desire for peace and harmonious coexistence, upon which individuals, as well as nations, must live right here on earth.

Perhaps we all may reflect that harmonious coexistence may come through sincere evaluation of motives and not through the building of another tower of Babel.

3. Is There Nothing Sacred?

God made a covenant with Abraham. This covenant was not only with Abraham alone but with all Jews of the future generations as an initiation of all Jews into a peoplehood and an active association with God.

The text reads, ". . . You shall keep my covenant. You and your offspring to come throughout the ages. Such shall be the covenant, which you shall keep, between Me and you and your offspring to follow: every male among you shall be circumcised . . . At the age of eight days, every male among you throughout the generations shall be circumcised . . . Thus shall My covenant be marked in your flesh as an everlasting pact." (*Genesis,* 17:9-13)

This bodily sign is the covenant by which Jews become part in a religious unity with God. As Maimonides states, "It gives to all members of the same faith, i.e., to all believers in the unity of God, a common bodily sign . . ." (Moses Maimonides, *The Guide to the Perplexed.* Part 3, Ch. 49)

Circumcision is considered the most important commandment of the Torah. (*Aruch Hashulchan,* Hilchot Mila Ch. 260:4) The law declares that the father is obligated to circumcise his son, if the father did not circumcise his son, the Bet Din (religious court) is obligated to circumcise him. In places where there is no Bet Din, the obligation to circumcise is placed upon every Jew of the town. If however, one grows up without being circumcised, he is obligated to circumcise himself. (*Ibid,* Ch. 261:1-3)

Circumcision has been observed by Jews throughout the ages with much more vehemence and zeal than any other ritual. As Rabbi Simeon B. Eleazer declared, "Every precept for which Israel submitted to death at the time of the royal decrees, such as idolatry and circumcision, is still firmly observed, whereas precepts for which Israel did not submit to death at the time of the royal decrees, such as tefillin, are still weak in their hands." (*Talmud Sabbath,* 130a.)

The traditional exercise of circumcision was very seldom attacked even by non-practicing Jews. Some enlightened Jews however, in the 19th Century considered circumcision to be no longer in keeping with the dictates of religious prescription.

Its abolition was advocated by the Friends of Reform (Reformfreunde) in Frankfort-on-the-Main in 1843. It caused a bitter con-

8

troversy in the Jewish community as David Einhorn and many Reform rabbis opposed the Frankfort Reform Verein . . . (*The Jewish Encyclopedia*, Vol. 4, p. 96)

Despite the universal acceptance of traditional circumcision among Jews, on rare occasion, one will rise, criticize, and demand new reform in the traditional practice.

In a recent article entitled "Ritual Circumcision, Covenants and Current Practices in American Hospitals," in *Clinical Pediatrics*, (vol. 1, no. 1, Oct. 1962), the author states that a personal survey conducted by him revealed that "accidents do frequently occur in the hands of Mohalim, but these are seldom reported in the medical literature or in Jewish sources."

The "Personal Survey" to which the author makes reference is another article written by him in *Jewish Social Studies*, (vol. 24, no. 1, January 1962) entitled "Worldwide Survey of the Current Practice of Mila (Circumcision)."

In addition to the methodological shortcomings of the survey, in no way has the author shown any frequency of accidents in the hands of the mohalim. It is most unfortunate that, in the name of science, one sets out himself to provide all the preconceived notions that one has about traditional circumcision.

The Jew performs this ritual not for any health or hygienic reasons. In fact, "No one should circumcise himself or his son for any other reason but for pure faith." (Maimonides, *Ibid.*)

The ritual of circumcision with the Jew is not something by or through which he becomes saved or purified. It is not that by which an individual becomes a Jew because according to the law one is a Jew even if he is not circumcised (*Shulchan Aruch*).

To the Jew the ritual of circumcision is a manifestation of making a bond with the God of Abraham. It is an entrance into a binding agreement and a symbolic relationship with God. It is a religious duty that binds, connects, and solidifies the individual with this group. It becomes the symbol of identity, belonging and cohesiveness.

As Maimonides further states, ". . . There is much mutual love and assistance among people that are united by the same sign when they consider it as the symbol of the covenant. Circumcision is likewise the symbol of the covenant which Abraham made in connection with the belief in God's unity and everyone that is circumcised enters the covenant of Abraham to believe in the unity of God,

9

in accordance with the words of the law 'to be a God unto thee, and to thy seed after thee'." (*Genesis* 17:7) (Maimonides, *Ibid.*)

Among Jews the practice of circumcision was and still is a religious ritual associated with holiness. Circumcision as a common bodily sign brings the individual Jew into the Covenant of Abraham and the unity of God. To the Jew circumcision is a holy ritual and does not deserve to be tampered with by pseudo-scientific surveys.

4. Must the Righteous Perish?

Abraham intervened with God's decree for the people of Sodom and Gomorrah. As God wanted to destroy these two cities, Abraham pleaded, "Will You sweep away the innocent along with the guilty? What if there should be 50 innocent within the city; will You then wipe out the place and not forgive it for the sake of the innocent 50 who are in it?

"Far be it from You to do such a thing to bring death upon the innocent as well as the guilty . . . Shall not the Judge of all the earth deal justly?"

The Lord answered, "If I find within the city of Sodom, 50 . . ., 45 . . . 40 . . . 30 . . . 20 . . . (or even) 10 . . . innocent men, I will not destroy for the sake of the 10." (*Genesis* 18:20-33)

This is an important lesson in moral-ethical value judgment:

(1) *The responsibility of one man caring for another*—Abraham was praying for the people of Sodom and Gomorrah thereby indicating that one man cannot remove himself when his fellow is in danger. One man cannot keep himself aloof just because he himself is unaffected. Human beings have a specific responsibility for each other. Individuals and societies are interdependent upon each other. The responsibility lies within every human being to care for his fellow.

(2) *Consideration for individual human values*—Abraham displayed humanitarian compassion by showing deep concern even for the sinners. Wickedness was so great in Sodom that even the practice of charity was strictly forbidden. The Midrash relates that a poor girl and a rich girl went to a well together to exchange vessels. The poor girl gave the wealthy one a jug of water and the wealthy one in return gave the poor girl a basket containing bread. When this be-

came known in the community of Sodom, both girls were burned alive. (*Yalkut, Genesis* 83, also, *Midrash Rabbah Genesis* 49:6) Despite this wickedness, Abraham pleaded for such people.

(3) *Deep concern for justice*—Abraham pleaded, "Far be it from God to bring death upon the innocent alike with the guilty . . ."

(4) *The impact of a righteous minority upon the entire community*—Ten righteous men were able to save an entire city.

Besides these moral-ethical implications, the text needs further elucidation. From the dialogue between God and Abraham it is apparent that God would not punish the righteous, but on the contrary, God would spare the wicked because of the righteous. This presents much conflict and inconsistency in the sad pages of Jewish history.

In every generation when misfortune and disaster befell the camps of Israel the cry went out: "Where is justice? Why must the righteous perish with the wicked?"

Can it be said that all those who perished during the destruction and evil design of the Nazis were wicked? It is mighty wrong to assume or claim that each time a calamity fell upon the house of Israel that all those who perished were guilty.

The "six million" martyrs who perished under Hitler were all innocent, most of them were righteous and many of them were holy and pure. Hence, the question: "Shall not the Judge of all the earth deal justly?"

This question has no answer! Nor is it fair to rationalize that any group of human beings ever deserved this kind of punishment.

When there is no adequate answer, at least, may the question be modified. Questions should not imply the answers to mean that God destroys the innocent alike with the wicked. Let the questions rather imply that it is far from God, to bring death upon the innocent as well as the guilty.

Midrash relates, "Rabbi Levy expounded that two men, Abraham and Job, said the same thing. Abraham said, 'Far be it from You to slay the righteous with the wicked,' and Job said: 'It is all one—therefore I say: He destroyed the innocent and the wicked.' (*Job* 9:22) Yet, Abraham was rewarded for it, whereas, Job was punished for it. The reason is because Abraham said it in confirmation (i.e. surely God is not so unjust as to slay the righteous . . .) While Job said it in cavil: 'It is all one . . .' " (*Midrash Rabbah, Genesis* 49:9).

Man has no adequate answer to why the innocent must perish.

11

At least let him temper and diminish the force and the harshness of the question. Let his questions be directed in a spirit of plea and prayer.

Far be it from You, O Lord, to slay the righteous with the wicked, because such an act is alien to Your nature. Far be it from You, O Lord, because such an act would only profane Your Divine Name. (*Ibid*)

5. "The Jewish Way of Death"

Jewish history began when Abraham took Sarah his wife and left the rich civilization of Ur of the Chaldees to go to the land of Canaan. Abraham and Sarah began together their active, difficult, and gratifying journey of life.

They were facing together the problems caused by Sarah's beauty . . . her childlessness . . . her jealousy about Hagar . . . the Lord's promise of a son . . . the birth of Isaac . . . the binding of Isaac upon the altar . . .

Now this wonderful partner of life, Sarah, died and Abraham came to mourn and weep for her.

Nowhere in the Torah do we find such a detailed description of funeral arrangements as with Sarah. The Torah devotes 20 verses in rendering the episode of the transaction between Abraham and Ephron the Hittite in obtaining the burial ground for Sarah.

The detailed description of the transaction may be a form of emphasizing the great loss and pain involved in the departure of one's wife.

As Rabbi Johanan states, "Every man whose first wife dies is considered as if the Holy Temple was destroyed in his lifetime." Alexandri said, "Every man whose wife dies is as if his whole world became darkened." (*Talmud Sanhedrin* 22a)

Despite the deep mourning, personal and emotional involvement about a person's passing, Jewish religion demands that life should continue uninterruptedly. Immediately after Sarah's funeral, Abraham sent Eliazer, his servant, to bring a wife for Isaac; because as soon as Sarah died another woman of the same calibre had to take her place to maintain the Jewish family life.

As the Talmud states, "No righteous person departs this world until a similar righteous person is created." (*Talmud Kidushin,* 72b)

In the Bible the death of Sarah is described after the birth of Rebecca has been announced. As the Midrash explains the meaning of the Ecclesiastics statement, "The sun rises and the sun goes down . . ." (*Eccl.* 1:5) Rabbi Abba said, "Do we not know that the sun rises and the sun goes down?"

But the meaning is that before the Holy One, blessed be He, causes the sun of one righteous man to set, he causes the sun of another righteous man to rise.

Thus on the day that Rabbi Akiba died Rabbi Judah the Prince (compiler of the Mishnah) was born . . . On the day Rabbi Judah the Prince died Rabbi Adda b. Ahabah was born . . . On the day that Rabbi Addah b. Ahabah died Rabbi Abin was born . . .

Before the Holy One, blessed be He, caused Moses' sun to set, He caused Joshua's sun to rise . . . Before Eli's sun set the sun of Samuel rose . . . Before the Holy One, blessed be He, allowed Sarah's sun to set He caused the sun of Rebecca's to rise. (*Midrash Rabbah Genesis*)

As families replace their outstanding members, so do communities reproduce their leaders generation after generation. In fact, one of the great contributing factors of Jewish survival lies in the ability to replace the leadership.

Every generation has its own Abraham and its own Moses. As the Midrash relates, "Rabbi said . . . there is no generation that does not contain men like Abraham and there is no generation which does not contain men like Jacob, Moses and Samuel." (*Midrash Rabbah Genesis,* 56.7)

Just because the pious and the righteous are replaceable and are usually immediately replaced, it does not mean that their departure can be taken casually. On the contrary, one must deeply mourn the passing of great men.

The Talmud relates, "Rabbi Hiyya bar Abba said in the name of Rabbi Johanan, 'He who is slothful to lament a sage will not prolong his days'." (*Talmud, Sabbath* 195b)

Furthermore, "Rabbi Simeon b. Pazzi said in the name of Rabbi Joshua b. Levi in Bar Kappara's name, 'If one sheds tears for a worthy man, the Holy One, blessed be He, counts them and lays them up in His treasure house . . .'" (*Ibid.*)

Jewish life demands a rational and balanced behavior with regard to mourning. Thus the law prescribes that one must not weep over the dead more than three days and must not mourn more than seven days. But for Torah scholars one may mourn in accordance with their knowledge and wisdom.

However, even for them one must not mourn beyond 30 days because even for Moses the children of Israel did not weep longer than 30 days.

Also those who do not mourn for their dead as prescribed by the rabbis are considered cruel and inappropriate according to the Torah . . . (*Aruch Hashulchan* 394)

Jewish mourning and funeral practices need much spiritual strengthening. It is unfortunate that Jewish traditional patterns that were once associated with dignity and deep emotional concern are replaced by commercialism.

Practices that were once associated with personal honor and respect are replaced by unnecessary expenditure as a means of paying for our own psychological anxiety and guilt.

In a society where the dead are handled by mortuary scientists, cosmeticians and hair dressers; where death business is based upon sophisticated profiteering and funeral paganism, Jewish communities should not add to this fad with additional ill-practices such as "catered funerals" and others.

Let the intelligent people take the initiative in bringing back some traditional meaning and religious values to that one practice which leads us all to the end of our way.

6. The Voice Is the Voice of Jacob ...

Isaac became old and wanted to bless his older son Esau before he died. Isaac called Esau and said, "Take your weapons, your quiver and your bow and go out to the field and hunt a game for me and prepare for me savory food, such as I love, and bring it to me, that I may eat, that I may bless you before I die." (Genesis 27:1-5)

Rebecca persuaded Jacob to impersonate his brother in order to receive the father's blessing. She prepared the food, put upon Jacob Esau's best garment, and skins of kids she placed upon his hands and his neck to make him appear hairy like Esau.

Jacob came unto his father and pretended to be Esau and said,

14

"I am Esau your first born. I have done as you told me; now pray, sit up and eat of my game, that you may bless me."

But Isaac suspecting that something was wrong, said, "How is it that you have found it so quickly . . . come near, that I may feel you, my son, whether you are really my son Esau or not."

Jacob came close, the father felt him and said, "The voice is Jacob's voice, but the hands are the hands of Esau." And Isaac did not recognize him because of the hairy hands, and blessed him . . .

Most of the commentators not only justify Jacob's action but do not even admit that receiving the blessing by Jacob was a deception. The text is very clear on the entire procedure of the blessing episode that Jacob pretended to be Esau, and that he did not tell the truth. Jacob specifically stated, "I am Esau your first-born."

On the other hand, if Jacob was meant to be the receiver of the blessing, why was he not asked by his father? Or, is it possible that this episode was to indicate the future lot of Jacob—that he is to receive blessing and life's privileges only through deception?

It would be most difficult to conceive of the notion that in order for Jacob to become successful in worldly pursuits, he has to achieve it only through devious means. Unfortunately, Jewish history affirms much of these and similar types of accusations.

It is, however, conceivable that Isaac himself was undecided which son should carry on the family line of Abraham. True, Esau had a claim because he was the first born. But, also, if Isaac was to follow the precedent established by his father, the family pedigree was to be carried by the younger son, as in the case of Isaac who, too, was the younger son, the junior of Ishmael.

The problem with this line of thinking is, however, that Abraham did not choose Isaac to follow in the ancestral line because he was the youngest son, the same way as Ishmael was not preferred to carry over the progenitorship of Abraham because he was the oldest son, or the first born of Abraham.

The determining factor for having the privilege or in carrying on Abraham's family lineage was not the *precedent* Abraham set with Isaac, nor was it the birthright of Esau. The criteria for the privilege of family pedigree lineage was a special merit, to be earned and deserved on a personal level, rather than on an ascribed factor.

Isaac has shown excellence by his willingness to be sacrificed as a burnt-offering before God and thereby merited the lineage of Abraham. Jacob being "a quiet man, dwelling in tents" has not performed any spectacular deed while living at home from which Isaac could have assumed any kind of approbation.

In fact, according to Rashi it was Esau who tried hard to impress his father about his righteous performances. Isaac needed some evidence by which Jacob could show his extraordinary devotion, dedication, and attachment.

In his eagerness for the blessing, Jacob exposed himself to censure, condemnation and contempt by his father and to hatred and to a possibility of being killed by his brother.

This devious act, so foreign to him, Jacob could not have done were he not moved by some higher, elevated and deeper meaning that he attached to his father's blessing and family lineage.

When Jacob entered to receive the blessing, Isaac said, "The voice is Jacob's voice, but the hands are the hands of Esau." In this stage of perplexity while performing successfully an act that is not becoming for a Jacob, Isaac indicated that he can receive the blessing only for one reason, and that is the "voice of Jacob."

Jacob may put himself into the garment of Esau, he may pretend to have the strong physique and the outdoor quality of Esau, but his real power, his real ability and his inner potentiality lies in the voice of Jacob. This is far more powerful than the hands of Esau.

As the Midrash tells (if one is interested in subjugating the people of Israel, he should) go to their houses of worship and houses of studies and if he finds there children with their voices uplifted he cannot subjugate them.

This is so because their forefather assured them that as long as the voice of Jacob rings out in the houses of prayer, Esau's hand has no dominion over them. (*Midrash Rabbah Genesis* 45:20)

Through the voice of Jacob, Isaac understood that behind this voice is plea, and prayer. Behind this voice is the voice of Israel of the future. Behind this voice is the spiritual power that moves the earthly and the heavenly, deserving of blessing.

But, now Esau came back from his hunt. He, too, prepared a tasty food and brought it to his father and asked his father to sit up and eat his game.

The Torah relates, *"Isaac was seized with a very violent trembling . . ."* He was pondering: Is it possible that I blessed the wrong person?

". . . that hunted game . . ." How could Jacob hunt game when nobody knew that skill besides Esau?

16

" . . . *and he brought it to me* . . ." How did it occur to his mind to bring it to me when I did not tell anyone besides Esau?

". . . *and I have eaten all* . . ." I ate more than I usually eat, and besides, the food tasted like the best delicacies in the world.

". . . *before you came* . . ." all these the hunting, the preparing, bringing and eating happened in such a great haste.

". . . *and I blessed him* . . ." I felt like blessing him and by so doing I felt comfortable.

"*Now he must remain blessed* . . ." Despite all these unusual circumstances, Isaac felt at ease in blessing Jacob. It seemed as though God consented to his blessing. Devious as the whole affair was, Isaac confirmed his blessing. (*Malbim*)

7. Jewish Dreams and Images

The unfavorable image of the Jew held by non-Jews throughout the ages is more or less known and recorded in Jewish history. The critical attitudes toward Jews by non-Jews in European countries, particularly in the past few decades, have been even experienced by many, and sadly remembered by all the Jewish communities throughout the world.

Unfavorable attitudes held about Jews in the United States are less known, but, fortunately, less intensified as well. A recent survey of cross-religious groups shows a diversified reaction with regard to the unfavorable attitudes held about Jews. (Gerhard Lenski, *The Religious Factor*, 1961). But despite the diversity, the score about the unfavorable image is, still, very low.

The question is asked, time and again, why are Gentiles critical of Jews? Although many reasons are being offered to explain or to justify the existence of the unfavorable attitudes, none of them really adequately explains the underlying causes of these attitudes.

The Jew maintained one specific character throughout the ages for which he was simultaneously envied and hated. He was a dreamer and dared to dream even at a time when dreaming was absurd.

Jewish history reveals that the Jew remained after other societies disappeared; that he continued to live much beyond the life and existence that was allotted to him by his enemies. He continued to compete for life and for survival under the most strenuous circumstances. He still exists today, performs and plays a role of no insignificance.

What is the secret behind his miraculous survival? What is the formula for his mysterious continuity?

The secret lies in his ability to dream!

The one factor that is most consistent about the Jew is that he never stopped dreaming. Throughout the ages the Jew has always been a dreamer. During slavery in Egypt he dreamed about freedom.

In the desert he dreamed about the Promised Land. In the *galut* he dreamed about the messiah. In the dark hours of our century he dreamed of an Israel.

If he was ignorant, he dreamed of a son, a scholar. If he was poor, he dreamed of a wealthy son. His aim was always high and he dreamed about the unattainable.

For the Jew failure was not a crime but aiming low was. When he reached the stage that was once his dream, he heightened his aspiration level and continued dreaming.

The Bible gives a full account of the dreams and accomplishments of a young man who was compelled to leave his parents' house and start a life on his own.

The text reads, "Jacob left Beersheba and went toward Haran. He came to a certain place and stopped there for the night, because the sun had set.

"Taking one of the stones of the place, he put it under his head and lay down in that place to sleep. And he dreamed that there was a ladder set on the ground and its top reached to heaven; and the angels of God were going up and down on it.

"And the Lord was standing beside him and said, '. . . The land on which you are lying I will give to you and your offspring. Your descendants shall be as the dust of the earth . . . Remember, I am with you: I will protect you wherever you go and will bring you back to this land . . .' " (*Genesis* 28:10-15)

This was the dream of Jacob and this became the dream of the children of Israel of the future. And ever since that time the Jew continued dreaming. In his dream, the Jew built a ladder that was standing on the ground and its top reached to heaven. In his dream, he constructed the means of overcoming the gap between the earthly and the heavenly.

He was dreaming of a ladder that provided for a free social mobility. On his ladder even angels were moving upward and down-

18

ward. His ladder reached heaven while he was still lying on the ground. He realized that he could reach heights only if he aimed high even at the time he was at a low ebb.

He put a stone under his head indicating that the lofty dreams, the high aims and ideals must be pursued even during time of discomfort and hardship. In his dream, Jacob spoke with God assuring him of security and protection and a continuity forever.

Yes, the Jew can change the unfavorable image of himself by non-Jews if he stops dreaming. As J. O. Hertzler says, ". . . To cease to be a cultural irritant the Jew must be completely assimilated. Any old sense of allegiance to his 'chosen people' idea will have to disappear; he must consciously remove characteristics of behavior which are recognizably Jewish; he must deliberately mold himself and his life on gentile patterns . . .

"He will have to be completely absorbed ethnically . . . He will have to give up all pride in his group and his people's history and denationalize himself as a Jew." (In Isacque Graeber and S. H. Britt [eds.] *Jews in a Gentile World*, 1942, p. 98-99).

This the Jew is neither willing nor able to do. And so, he will go on dreaming lofty dreams, about the ladder set on the ground and its top reaching to heaven.

8. When Jacob Stands Alone...

One of the basic requirements for adequate personality is to maintain a close association with one's group. When a man separates himself from the group, he lacks the strong conviction of his own worth. His inability to make contact with others may be due to a destructive attitude and hostility. (C. Thompson, "An Introduction to Minor Maladjustment," *The American Handbook of Psychiatry*, pp. 239-240).

Social difficulties, also, emerge as the individual moves into isolation and aloneness. As one's separation grows, so does his intensity of insecurity. An individual's makeup is so constructed that in order to enjoy an affirmative reciprocal relationship with others, he must develop identification and association with groups.

Group relationship provides the individual with strength and courage to face all problems that life is to bring about. It provides a feeling of security in knowing that the problems are not faced alone, but shared with others.

This conception has been further developed by Emile Durkheim (1858-1917) a French sociologist. He considered that a unified, highly integrated group develops a set of norms to regulate behavior and interpersonal relations.

The group provides the individual with a sense of security by establishing clearly defined codes of what is proper and improper for all the people within the group (Leonard Broom and Philip Selznick, *Sociology*, 1963, pp. 29-30).

In Jewish life, also, the association with the group provides the Jew with his basic values. Consequently, the person who becomes a *poresh min hatzibur*—one who severs his relationship from the Jewish community—is considered one of the most severe deviants.

A brief passage of the Zohar reflects upon the serious and harsh consequences that result from removing oneself from his group.

The Bible relates that Jacob was very much afraid because Esau came with 400 men to meet him. He divided the people, the flocks and the herds into two camps. That night Jacob took his family, his wives, and children, and his personal belongings over the stream.

"And (as) Jacob was left alone, a spirit wrestled with him until the break of dawn." (*Genesis* 32:4-27). The Zohar adds, although Jacob was beloved by the Almighty, yet when he was left alone, a strange spirit immediately came and joined battle with him. (Zohar 169 b).

This is to signify that when Jacob *stands alone* without his group; when he removes himself from his group, regardless of his rank, a strange spirit joins battle with him. Without the support of the group the external influence wrestles with him until the very end . . .

The same is true with any Jew. As long as he associates and identifies with the larger group, he has personal security and attachment. But once the Jew stands alone, he must wrestle with all the external forces.

History, too, has demonstrated that the threat to Jewish continuity begins when Jews separate themselves from their groups. Because as long as Jews continue to be members of Jewish groups and associate with other Jews, regardless of their indifference to religious rituals, they cannot and will not assimilate.

This holds true even today. The various groups and denominations in Judaism do not stand alone. They are culturally interdependent upon each other.

The words of the Zohar still convey deep meaning of significance even today. "When Jacob is left alone a strange spirit immediately comes and joins battle with him." The individual Jew can be overtaken spiritually, and annihilated culturally *only when he stands alone,* away from his group and brethren.

There are the many signs that Jews do not stand alone but depend upon each other. They join, unite, and consolidate in matters of culture, and thereby they generate a more intensive group cohesiveness in order to retain self identification.

9. And They Hated Him ...

The mere physical ability of parenthood does not necessarily make one into a good or adequate parent. Many family situations do not make a home very conducive to an ideal family life. Personality maladjustments are usually closely related to early family life.

In addition to the proper presentation of values, ideals, ethics and social habits which make the family the basic training ground for society, the home must also provide a reasonable, happy and secure base for living for each and every individual member of the family.

In recent years the need for gratification of every individual in the family has been recognized by students of social science (James H. S. Bossard, *The Sociology of Child Development,* 1954).

The Bible describes a family life in which discrimination of affection is shown. In this family the father shows favoritism to one of his sons, which makes the others envious and hateful.

It portrays a family in which (one of) the younger brothers has dreams of grandeur to become the leader over the others and place them in a subordinate position. For this the brothers' dislike grows into ill-will and hate to the point that they even contemplate killing him.

What could lead to such hatred? What could a brother do to generate in the others such anger as to be ready even to kill?

The text reads, ". . . Israel loved Joseph best of all his sons, for he was the child of his old age; and he had made him a coat of many colors. And when his brothers saw that their father loved him more than any of his brothers, *they hated him* . . .

"Joseph had a dream which he told his brothers; and *they hated him even more.* He said to them, 'Hear this dream which I have dreamed: In it we were binding sheaves in the field, when suddenly my sheaf stood up and remained upright; then your sheaves gathered around and bowed low to my sheaf.'

"His brothers answered, 'Do you mean to reign over us? Do you mean to rule over us?' And *they hated him even more* for his talk about his dreams." (*Genesis* 37:3-8).

The text repeats *"they hated him"* three times, indicating three basic reasons for their hate.

First, they hated him because the father showed favoritism toward Joseph. This favoritism was not only an inward psychological manifestation, but a conscious overt expression. The father made a marked distinction between Joseph and his brothers by giving him a coat of many colors—a clear distinction of status.

This was not necessarily Joseph's fault, it was a situation the father created, perhaps because of his own psychological involvement: (a) Joseph was the son that reminded him most of his beloved wife, Rachael (b) Jacob identified himself with Joseph because Joseph resembled him physically the most. As Rabbi Judah said, ". . . *son of his old age"* means that Joseph's physical features (*ziv ikunim*) resembled Jacob's (*Midrash Rabbah Genesis* 84:8); (c) Jacob was able to further identify with Joseph because of the similarity of circumstances.

As the Midrash said, ". . . As Jacob's brother hated him, so did the brothers of Joseph; as Jacob's brother sought to kill him, so did the brothers of Joseph; as Jacob was promoted through his dream, so was Joseph . . ." (*Ibid* 84:6).

The second reason for the brothers hating Joseph was because he dreamed and in his dreams he took advantage of his father's favoritism. He interpreted the father's differential treatment to mean that he could place his brothers in a subordinate position.

Again, it may be pointed out that the dreams, too, could be the result of the conditions created by his father's discrimination of affection.

The third reason for the brothers hating Joseph, perhaps the most damaging to their relationship, was the fact that Joseph told them about the dreams.

22

He could have been much more sensitive in recognizing that the father's differential treatment of his brothers was very much resented by them. But instead, Joseph, being the father's favorite, was ostentatiously flaunting his dreams.

Although the episode of Joseph and his brothers—selling him and his becoming an important figure in Egypt—is an important antecedent to the fate and the history of the Children of Israel in their achieving nationhood, it must be recognized that the hatred generated among his brothers was not necessarily justifiable. It was wrong to show favoritism and differential treatment.

It seems that the Midrash recognized this problem, as it clearly states, ". . . and he made him a coat of many colors . . ." Resh Lakish said in the name of Rabbi Eleazer ben Azariah: "A man must not make a distinction among his children, for on account of the coat of many colors which our ancestor Jacob made for Joseph they hated him." (Ibid 84:8).

While history has its peculiarities in its continuity and development, as we examine its processes, let us recognize its flaws. Man must cultivate values that consider any behavior that generates dissension and hatred as morally wrong and evocative of men's strong resentment of every generation.

10. I Shall Be Superior to You . . .

Joseph was called upon to interpret Pharaoh's dream that no one in Egypt was able to explain satisfactorily. In addition, he advised Pharaoh to place a "discerning and wise man" over the land of Egypt who would appoint officers to direct the internal affairs of the land.

Pharaoh was very much pleased with Joseph's advice and interpretation of his dream. He said to the courtiers, "Could we find another like him, a man in whom is the spirit of God?"

And Pharaoh said to Joseph, "Since God has made all this known to you, there is none so discerning and wise as you. You shall be in charge of my court, and by your command shall all my people be directed; only with respect to the throne shall I be superior to you." (Genesis 41:37-41).

And thus Joseph was put in charge not only of the royal household but of the whole administration.

23

It was not strange in this culture for a slave to reach such a high position because Syrian slaves were frequently elevated to such dignities. (Adolf Erman, *Life in Ancient Egypt*, tr. H. M. Tirard, 1894, pp. 106-7, 517-18).

Joseph's aggressiveness, however, caused some concern to Pharaoh. He recognized Joseph as an extremely ambitious man who would have an important role in the life of Egypt. He, thus, willingly offered him the second highest ranking position of the land.

But at the same time Pharaoh felt threatened by Joseph's ambition. At the very outset of the appointment Pharaoh made clear that he would remain superior to him. He said to Joseph, "You shall be in charge over my court . . . (yet) with respect to the throne I shall be superior to you."

The Midrash draws a most interesting parallel between God and Pharaoh. As Pharaoh warned Joseph that he would remain superior to him, so did God warn Israel that He shall remain greater and holier than they.

The Midrash reads, "Resh Lakish said, 'Two things our teacher Moses stated in the Torah and we learn their meaning from the passage about that wicked man Pharaoh'."

(1) And the Lord will make you the head . . . (*Deuteronomy* 28:13). "You might actually think like Myself: Therefore, *'rak'* is inserted to mean, My greatness will be higher than your greatness. Now we learn this interpretation from the present passage, 'You shall be in charge over my court, and by your command shall all my people be directed. Yet lest you should think, that you will be as great as I, it states, 'only (rak) with respect to the throne will I be superior to you.' My greatness is above yours."

Again, (2) "Speak unto the Congregation of the Children of Israel and say unto them: You shall be holy . . . (*Leviticus* 19:2) Lest you should think, like Myself, the text adds, *'For I the Lord your God am holy* . . . My holiness is above your holiness.' Now this interpretation we learn from the passage about this wicked Pharaoh: 'And Pharaoh said unto Joseph. "I am Pharaoh" ' for lest you should think that you will be as great as I, it says 'I am Pharaoh,' meaning that my greatness is above yours." (*Midrash Rabbah Genesis* 80:2).

The indications are that just as Joseph did not reach the greatness of Pharaoh, so in Jewish life no man can ever reach such heights as to replace the functions or surpass the holiness of God. Jewish theology considers God as the continuous creator of the world. He does not take a passive role of a disinterested spectator.

According to the Talmud, God presides over the births of man . . . (*Niddah* 31a); He takes care that the race shall not die out . . . (*Pesahim* 43b); He is the power of and the will behind the acts of terrestrial governments (*Ecclesiastes Rabbah* 10:11); God sends the wind that the farmer may have wherewith to live . . . (*Leviticus Rabbah* 28).

God is very much involved in the continuous direction of the affairs of the universe. In fact, the Talmud does not consider the creation as ever being finished, (*Hagigah* 12a) as is stated in the Morning Prayers, "The Lord . . . renews the creation every day continuously."

11. "I Am Joseph Your Brother"

There was famine in the land and the children of Israel went down to Egypt to buy food. When Joseph saw his brothers he recognized them but they did not recognize him. Joseph spoke to them harshly and accused them of spying.

He insisted that they bring Benjamin with them on their next trip to Egypt. With great difficulty, Judah persuaded his father to let Benjamin go; and so they came to Egypt.

Joseph instructed his house steward to fill his brothers' sacks with food, to return each one's money, and to put Joseph's silver goblet into the sack of Benjamin.

As soon as they left the city, Joseph sent men after his brothers who searched them and found the goblet in Benjamin's bag. They returned to the city and threw themselves before Joseph.

Joseph said to them, "What is this deed that you have done?"

Judah replied, "What can we say to my lord? . . . Here we are, then, slaves of my lord, the rest of us as much as he in whose possession the goblet was found."

But Joseph said, "Far be it from me to act like this! Only he in whose possession the goblet was found shall be my slave; the rest of you may go back unhindered to your father."

Now Judah began to plead, "Please my lord, let your servant appeal . . . My lord asked his servants, 'Have you a father or

25

another brother?' We told my lord, 'We have an old father and there is a child of his old age . . . he alone is left of his mother . . .' Then you said to (us), 'Bring him down to me . . .' We said to (you), 'The boy cannot leave his father; if he were to leave him, his father would die . . .' But you said to (us), 'Unless your youngest brother comes down with you, do not let me see your faces . . .' Later our father said, 'Go back and procure some food for us.' We answered, 'We cannot go down unless our youngest brother is with us.'

"My father said to us, 'As you know, (Rachel) bore me two sons. But one is gone torn by a beast! . . . If you take this one from me too, and he meets with disaster, you will send my white head down to the grave in grief.' "

Now, Judah continued, "If I come . . . to my father and the boy is not with us—since his own life is so bound with his . . . he will die, and (we) will send the white head of . . . our father down to the grave in grief."

In addition, Judah pleaded, "(I) have pledged myself for the boy to my father saying, 'If I do not bring him back to you, I shall stand guilty before my father forever.' Therefore, please let me remain as a slave . . . instead of the boy, and let the boy go back with his brothers, O, how can I go back to my father without the boy? Let me not be witness to the woe that would overtake my father." (*Genesis* 43:18-34)

This is one of the most beautiful pleas and moving episodes in the Bible. Besides the emotional impact and the historical sequence of the story of Joseph and his brothers, this passage displays the true character of the children of Israel.

In these words the distinctive features of the 12 tribes of Israel are so beautifully emerging. Also, it seems evident that some of the specific traits symbolize the image of the 12 tribes of Israel of the future.

The following may be considered:

1. Brotherhood—True brotherhood is shown as all the brothers returned to the city and asked to be imprisoned the same way as the accused brother. The tribes of Israel were moved by the spirit of unity and peace.

This is later symbolized as written, "And He was King in Jeshurun, when the heads of people assembled, the tribes of Israel together." (*Deuteronomy* 33:5)

26

Rashi quoting the *Sifre* adds, "God is their King when they are gathered together in one group and peace and strife is among them."

2. Self-sacrifice—Self-sacrifice is shown as Judah pleads before Joseph to be allowed to remain a slave instead of his brother. This is later beautifully symbolized as related in the Talmud:

"When Israel stood at the sea, the tribes strove with one another, each wishing to jump into the sea first. Then came forward the tribe of Benjamin and jumped into the sea." (*Talmud*, Sotah 36b-37a)

3. Justice—Justice is shown by the diametrically opposing positions they took in settling matters. They sold a brother into slavery, on the one hand, and were asking to be put into prison to save a brother, on the other.

Brothers with this compassion could not sell a brother for malice, but only as their interpretation of justice. This is later symbolized as related in the Midrash: "Why did God give the crown to Judah (meaning that the royal house of David descended from him)? Surely he was not the only brave one of his brothers. Were not Simeon and Levi and the others valiant, too? But because he dealt justly with Tamar did he become the judge of the world." (See *Midrash Rabbah Exodus* 30:19 and Scripture *Genesis* 38:1-30).

4. Strong association with the father is shown by the extreme concern they manifested for the father's feelings. The father is the magnifying symbol. He provides the authority and leadership for the generations ahead.

He is the source of the family lineage for the ongoing generation. The father is the symbol of the continuity of tradition. This is depicted in the Talmud:

"When Israel sinned in the wilderness, Moses stood before God and uttered many prayers and supplications before Him, and he was not answered. Yet when he exclaimed, 'Remember Abraham, Isaac and Israel thy servants!' (*Exodus* 32:13) he was immediately answered." (*Talmud Sabbath* 30a)

Even in later generations the *zechut avot*—the merit of the fathers—remained the major proponent for the Divine grace. As the Talmud relates:

When Solomon built the Temple he desired to take the Ark into the Holy of Holies, whereupon the gates clave to each other. Solomon uttered 22 prayers, yet he was not answered.

"He exclaimed, 'Lift up your heads, O ye gates, . . . and the King of Glory shall come in. Who is this King of Glory? The Lord of Hosts. He is the King of Glory.' (*Psalms* 26).

"Yet he was not answered. But as soon as he prayed, 'O Lord, turn not away the face of your anointed, remember the good deeds of David your servant,' he was immediately answered." (*Talmud Sabbath* 20a).

When Joseph left home he hardly knew his brothers. He was too young to realize and appreciate the qualities of his brothers who were much older and more mature than he. Here in Egypt he really came to know them.

The last episode and Judah's plea clarified and proved to him his brothers' integrity, their earnest love for one another, their willingness for self-sacrifice, and their deep concern for the old father.

Now after all these facts have been revealed to him the Torah continues, "Joseph could no longer control himself before all the attendants and cried out, 'have everyone withdraw from me' "; i.e., he could no longer continue to play the role of the stern executive in front of the Egyptians; he could no longer pretend to be the harsh and heartless Egyptian, of Pharaoh's equal.

He broke down and said, "I am Joseph! Is my father still alive?"; i.e., is his spirit and influence still living with all of us brothers? "Come closer to me . . . let us no longer be estranged."

"I am Joseph your brother . . ."; i.e. I do want to identify myself as your brother despite the great honor I have in Egypt, I am still one of you, the Jew, Israel's son, your brother . . . (*Genesis* 45:1-4)

"And the brothers came to Jacob and they told him all the words of Joseph . . . and the spirit of Jacob their father revived." (*Ibid* 45:25-28).

12. Belief, Culture and Unity

As Jewish life is being transmitted continuously from one generation to another, it is essential that three basic principles are upheld: (1) Belief in one God; (2) Continuity of culture; and (3) Unity or group cohesion.

As the Jewish *mishpacha*—household or "clan" system—was transposed into a tribal organization, remarkable emphasis is placed on these principles.

(1) The belief in one God—"Before he died, Jacob called his 12 sons and said, 'Come together that I may tell you what is to befall you in days to come'." (*Genesis* 49:1).

The Midrash adds, "As Jacob was departing he said to his children, 'Is the God of Israel in heaven your Father? Maybe in your hearts you wish to break away from the Holy One, blessed be He?'

" 'Hear O Israel, our father,' they replied, 'as there is no desire in your heart to break away from God, so is there none in our hearts, but the Lord is our God, the Lord is one.' He (Jacob) too, thereupon made utterance with his lips saying 'Blessed be the name of His glorious kingdom for ever and ever'." (*Midrash Rabbah Genesis* 93:4).

(2) The continuity of culture—Jacob continued to transmit the tradition where his father, Isaac, left off. As the Midrash states, "When Isaac blessed Jacob he said to him, 'And God Almighty bless you . . .' (*Genesis* 28:3)

"With what did he conclude? 'And Isaac called Jacob and blessed him . . .' (*Ibid.*) So Jacob, too, began where his father left off, as it says, 'And Jacob called his sons . . .' (*Ibid.* 49:1)

"And when he blessed he concluded with the phrase *vezot*—'and this' i.e. 'and *this is* what their father said to them.' At the point where Jacob left off, Moses began, *vezot* i.e. 'and *this is* the blessing . . .' (*Deuteronomy* 33:1)

"With what did Moses conclude? With 'happy art thou Israel . . .' (*Ibid.* 33:29) And so David, too, when he came to utter praises he began where Moses left off, 'Happy is the man . . .' (*Psalms* 1:1)" (*Midrash Rabbah Genesis* 100:12)

(3) Unity and group cohesion—The conclusion of Jacob's blessing reads, "All these were the tribes of Israel 12 in number," not more and not less, which formed the tribal unity. The representation of 12 was necessary in most future activities in Israel.

Under the mountain Moses built an altar and 12 pillars according to the 12 tribes in Israel. (*Exodus* 24:4)

The stones of the breast plate of the High Priest shall be according to the names of the children of Israel, 12 according to their names . . . they shall be for the 12 tribes. (*Ibid.* 28:21)

For the symbolic representation in the Jordan River, the Lord said to Joshua, "Take 12 men, one out of every tribe . . ." (*Joshua* 4:1-9; see further references I *Kings* 18:31; Ezra 6:17; 8:35; Ezekiel 48:31)

Although the 12 tribes were blessed individually, they constituted one basic unit. The tribes were separately represented in community affairs, nonetheless, they were part of the entire group.

The great emphasis that is placed on unity in Jewish life is illustrated in the Midrash: "As long as Jews form one cohesive unit, even if idol worship is prevalent among them, the strictness of Divine justice cannot touch them." (*Midrash Tanchuma Shoftim* 18)

It seems that immediately after Jacob's death maintaining tribal unity was the great problem out of the above mentioned three basic principles.

While living, Jacob was the unifying factor in the family. However, after he died the brothers' distrust of Joseph grew considerably. Even Joseph changed his behavior with the brothers.

The Torah states, "When Joseph's brothers saw that their father was dead . . ." Rashi explains, the brothers recognized Joseph's changed behavior. During Jacob's lifetime Joseph had them at his table, out of deference to his father, but he did not invite them after his father's death.

The brothers were much concerned saying, "What if Joseph seeks to pay back for all the wrong we did him." And so "his brothers went to him and flung themselves before him and said, 'We are prepared to be your slaves . . .' " (*Genesis* 50:15-18)

Perhaps this may give rise to reflect upon our own individual family relationship. As long as the unifying force, the father or the mother are living, many families keep together out of deference to them. However, after they are gone, many families separate, divide and create a rift in their relationship.

Thus, the oneness of God, the continuity of culture, and group unity have been the strengthening factors in Israel's perpetuity.

II. From
THE BOOK OF EXODUS

13. The Bush Was Not Consumed

The second book of the Torah, in Hebrew is called *Shemot,* literally, "names" after the second word of the verse. In English it is called *Exodus* meaning "departure," which title comes through the Vulgate from the Septuagint.

The book of *Exodus* narrates the departure of the children of Israel, which have now become a people from Egypt. The Torah relates that Jacob and his children came to Egypt because Joseph was a high-ranking official there and was able to help them settle in the province of Goshen.

After the Hyksos monarchy fell (c.1600 BCE) under the new rulers or pharaohs, the position of the Hebrews deteriorated more and more, until they were reduced to serfdom. Their individuality was preserved, not only by their common origin, but also by the fact of the survival of their ancestors' spiritual ideals. Their faith stood out in great contrast to the polytheism of their masters. (Cecil Roth, *A Bird's-Eye View of Jewish History,* 1954, p. 5)

The Hebrews were oppressed by forced labor imposed upon them by a new Pharaoh who desired to destroy them as he demanded that all male children be thrown into the river.

Pharaoh's daughter found a Hebrew male child in the river whom she called "Moses" and adopted him. When Moses grew up he sympathized with his brethren and their sufferings. He slew an Egyptian overseer and had to flee the country. He went to Midian, became a shepherd to the priest Jethro and married his daughter Zipporah.

As Moses was feeding the sheep on Mount Horeb he had a marvelous experience. God appeared to him in a "blazing fire out of a thorn-bush (which was) all aflame, yet the bush was not consumed . . . God called to him . . . and said, 'I am the God of your father, the God of Abraham, the God of Isaac, and the God of Jacob . . . You shall free My people, the Israelites from Egypt'." (*Exodus* 3:1-10).

God's revelation to Moses was the beginning of the religious peoplehood of Israel. It is most remarkable that at this initial revelation God appeared through a burning bush. It seems to symbolize not only personal requirements necessary for religion, but also fundamental principles upon which Judaism is based.

The following are supported by the Midrash:

1. Inspiration—*Hitlahavut*—In a flame of fire—"to inspire Moses so that when he came to Sinai and saw the fire ('Sinai was on smoke because the Lord descended upon it on fire') he should be accustomed to it." (*Midrash Rabbah Exodus* 3:5)

2. Heart or wholeheartedness—*Leb Sholem*—In a flame (*labat*) of fire—"the fire was from both sides of the bush and upwards, just as the heart (*leb*) is placed between both sides of a man and his upper part" (*Ibid*) indicating that revelation must take place in the heart.

3. Belief in the omnipresence of God—*Emunah*—Out of the midst of the bush . . . "A heathen once asked Rabbi Joshua Ben-Karha, 'Why did God choose a thorn-bush from which to speak to Moses?' He replied, 'Were it a carob tree or a sycamore tree, you would have asked the same question; but to dismiss you without any reply is not fair, so I will tell you why. To teach you that no place is devoid to God's presence, not even a thornbush'." (*Ibid*)

4. Humility—*Anavah* and *Shiflut*—". . . the Schechinah descended and spoke with Moses from the midst of a thorn-bush . . . Rabbi Eliezer said, 'Just as the thorn-bush is the lowliest of all trees in the world, so Israel was lowly and humble in Egypt,' Therefore did God reveal Himself to them and redeem them, as it is said, And I come down to deliver them from Egypt'." (*Ibid*).

5. Hope, Confidence and Trust—*Bitachon*—"Rabbi Jose said, 'Just as the thorn-bush is the prickliest of all trees, . . . so was the servitude in Egypt more grievous before God than all other servitudes in the world . . .' (Also in all other generations) the pain and servitude of Israel is known to God, as it is said, 'I am surely mindful (*raoh roiti*) of their sufferings'." (*Ibid.*)

6. Fence—*Geder* or *Seyog*—"Rabbi Johanan said, 'Just as one makes of thorns a fence for a garden, so Israel is a fence for the world' " (*Ibid.*) (for it provides principles for justice, righteousness, and morality through its teachings).

7. Torah—"Just as the thorn-bush grows near any water, so Israel grew only in virtue of the Torah that is called water (*Talmud Baba Kama* 17b, 82b; *Aboda Zarah* 5a; *Genesis Rabbah* 84:15) as it is said, 'Everyone that thirsteth, come ye for water'." (*Isa.* 55:1) (*Ibid.*)

8. Two Worlds—*Olam Hazeh* and *Olam Habah*—"Just as thorns grow in the garden and by the river, so Israel participates both in this world and the world to come." (*Ibid.*)

9. Responsibility—*Arovut* or *Achrayut*—"Just as the thorn-bush produces thorns and roses, so among Israel are the righteous and wicked." (*Ibid.*) The two make up the house of Israel in which one is responsible for the other.

10. Proclaiming the Oneness of God—"*Leman Daat*"—"Rabbi Pinehas Ben-Hama the priest said, 'Just as when a man puts his hand into a thorn-bush, he does not at first feel it, but when he takes it out it scratches (for the thorns are bent downwards and only grip the hand when he takes it out) so when Israel came into Egypt no one perceived them, but when they went out, they departed with signs and wonders (proclaiming the Oneness of God)'." (*Ibid.*)

11. Eternity of Israel—*Nitzhiyut*—This perhaps should provide the Jew with the greatest encouragement. As the Midrash relates, "Why did God show Moses such a symbol (as the burning bush)? Because Moses had thought to himself that the Egyptians might consume Israel; hence did God show him a fire which burnt but did not consume, saying to him, 'just as the thorn-bush is burning and is not consumed, so the Egyptians will not be able to destroy Israel'." (*Ibid.*)

14. "My Name ... I Did Not Make Known"

The Children of Israel grew into a peoplehood during the 210 years they lived in Egypt. They were all Egyptian-born and thoroughly exposed to a culture of witchcraft. As the Talmud states, "Ten *kabs* (liquid measure) of witchcraft descended to the world, nine were taken by Egypt and one by the rest of the world." (*Talmud Kidushin* 49b)

Furthermore, Jews were many generations removed from Jacob and the 12 tribal patriarchs. There were many among them who assimilated into the Egyptian culture. As the Midrash states, "When Joseph died (many) gave up the practice of circumcision because they said, 'Let us become like the Egyptians'." (*Midrash Tanchuma,* Shemot 5.)

35

Now God said to Moses, "I have surely seen the affliction of My people that are in Egypt and have heard their cry . . . and I have come down to rescue them from the Egyptians . . . Therefore, I will send you to Pharaoh and you shall free My people the Israelites, from Egypt . . ." (*Exodus* 3:7-11)

Moses realized that the people who were that far removed from God and religion might be difficult to approach. Most people in those days were idolaters. They believed in man's power to direct the influences of the heavenly bodies. Moses now claiming the authority of a prophet was deeply concerned that the people would not believe in him.

Hence, he said to God, "When I come to the Israelites you say to them, 'The God of your forefathers has sent me to you,' and they ask me, 'What is His name?' what shall I say to them?" (*Exodus* 3:13)

And God said to Moses, *Ehyeh Asher-Ehyeh*—"I Am That I Am," i.e. I am with them in this trouble and I will be with them in the bondage of other kingdoms. (*Talmud Berakot* 9)

I am the Lord that redeems them now, and will redeem them always. I am the Lord that is God in this generation and in all generations to come. I Am because I Am. God is not the cause of something external of Himself, but He is the "Unmoved Mover" Whose existence is determined by His Being. (*Abarbanel,* Shemot 15)

The text reads, "And God spoke to Moses saying . . . 'And I appeared unto Abraham, Isaac and Jacob . . .' " The Midrash adds, "God said to Moses, 'Oh for those that are gone and cannot be replaced. Many times did I reveal Myself to Abraham, Isaac and Jacob as God Almighty but I did not make known unto them that My name is Lord (the tetragrammaton, the *Shem ha-meforash,* the *namen proprium* of God, which does not denote any attribute of God, nor does it imply anything except His existence) as I have told you, and still they did not doubt in My ways'."

The forefathers, too, had reasons to doubt in God. For example, the Midrash continues, "To Abraham (God) said, 'Arise, walk about the land, through its length and its breadth, for I give it to you.' (*Genesis* 13:17) Yet when he wanted to bury Sarah he found no plot of ground until he had purchased one; still he did not doubt in My ways.

"I said to Isaac, 'Reside in this land . . . I will give all these lands to you and your offspring . . .' (*Ibid.* 26:3). Yet when he

36

sought water to drink, he found none; instead, 'And the herdsmen of Gerar quarreled with Isaac's herdsmen saying, "The water is ours!' " (*Ibid.* 26:20) Yet he did not doubt in My ways.

"I said to Jacob, 'The ground on which you are lying I will give to you and your offspring.' (*Ibid.* 28:13) Yet when he sought a place to pitch his tent, he found none until he purchased one for 100 *kesitah* (*Ibid.* 34:19) and still he did not doubt in My ways, nor did he ask Me, as you have asked Me, what is My name . . ." (*Midrash Rabbah Exodus* 4:4)

It must be understood, however, that upon God's appearance to Moses lies the basic divine revelation of God to the children of Israel of all times. It was not necessary for God to appear to the patriarchs in the fullest form of revelation because they were not commanded to prophecy. There is no prophecy associated with God's appearance to the patriarchs.

As Maimonides states, "Abraham, Isaac and Jacob, or any other person before them did not tell the people, 'God said unto me, you shall do this and this . . .' God spoke to them on matters that were specifically related to them. He communicated to them things relating to their personal perfection, directed them in what they should do, and foretold them what the condition of their descendants would be; but nothing beyond this. They guided their fellow-men by means of argument and instruction." (Maimonides, *The Guide of the Perplexed*, M. Friedlander trans. Hebrew Publishing Co., pp. 236-240)

Unlike Moses, they were not commanded to address the people.

The great revelation was made to Moses because he was the greatest prophet in Israel and was commanded to go to the Children of Israel and speak to them.

Thus Maimonides continues, "When God appeared to Moses and commanded him to address the people and to bring them the message, Moses replied that he might first be asked to prove the existence of God in the universe and only after doing so he would be able to announce to them that God had sent him.

"For all men, with a few exceptions, were ignorant of the existence of God, their highest thoughts did not extend beyond the heavenly sphere, its forms or its influences. They could not yet emancipate themselves from sensation, and had not yet attained to any intellectual perfection.

"Then God taught Moses how to teach them and how to establish amongst them the belief in the existence of Himself, namely by

37

saying, *Ehyeh Asher-Ehyeh* . . . He is 'the Existing Being,' whose existence is absolute. The proof which he (Moses) was to give consisted in demonstrating that there is a Being of absolute existence, that has never been and never will be without existence." (*Ibid.*)

15. Indigence, Affluence and Anxieties

Life is constantly probing whether or not under challenging conditions an independent nation, or any other type of independent group, can maintain itself and its identity. There are three types of tests through which the endurance of peoples and groups are measured:

1. *The test of indigence* measures whether or not the group is able to endure economic insufficiencies, unpleasant social conditions, depressions, and being subordinated to superior forces.

2. *The test of affluence* measures whether or not a group is able to endure and maintain itself under favorable social conditions and an abundance of goods and services that society provides.

3. *The test of psychological stress* measures whether or not the group is able to endure fears and anxieties, frayed nerves, the internal pressures which are brought about by life's complexities.

As soon as the Jews became an entity as a social group, life's circumstances tested whether or not they could maintain themselves as a group. It seems they successfully withstood the test of indigence. (Moshe Sofer, *Torat Moshe*, vol. 2, pp. 31-32). The Jews in Egypt, enduring slavery, as the Egyptians "made their lives bitter with hard service in mortar and in brick, and in all manner of service in the field . . ." (Exodus 1:14) did not change their Jewish names nor the Hebrew language (Yalkut Shemuni, chap. 226). Thus, despite the unfavorable conditions, depression and subordination, they maintained their group identity.

The findings of the test of affluence is more doubtful. Before the children of Israel came out from Egypt, God said to Moses:

> Speak, I beg thee, in the ears of the people and let them ask every man of his neighbor, and every woman of her neighbor, jewels of silver, and jewels of gold . . . (Exodus 11:2)

The rabbis explain that the reason God begged Moses to ask for jewelry was because He did not want Abraham to complain that He kept only part of the promise in which He said:

> Thy seed shall be a stranger in a land that . . . shall serve them; and . . . shall afflict them four hundred years . . . But also that nation, whom they shall serve, will I judge; and afterward shall they come out with great wealth . . . (Genesis 15:13-14)

Therefore, God wanted Israel to take with them gold and silver to fulfill the second part of His promise. (Rashi, *Ibid,* 11:2)

The possession of gold and silver was the test of affluence, or as it is called the "test of the rich," trying the Jews to see whether or not they would remain loyal and maintain self identification despite great wealth (Moshe Sofer, *Ibid.*) If we judge from Moses' complaint:

> But Israel waxed fat, and kicked . . . And he forsook God who made him . . . (Deuteronomy 32:15)

they did not do too well in the face of affluence.

What about the test of psychological stress? The Jews on Passover are commanded to eat "bread of affliction because in *haste* did (they) come out of the land of Egypt." (Deuteronomy 16:3). In fact they were escaping as it is written, "And it was told the King of Egypt that the people *fled."* (Exodus 14:5). The question has been asked: From whom were they running? After all, Pharaoh gave them permission to go, as he said, "Rise up, get out from among my people, both ye and the children of Israel, go and serve the Lord . . ." (Exodus 12:31). From whom were the Jews running? The answer is given that they were running from themselves. (See Shlomo Joseph Zein, Le Torah v'le Moadim, p. 352).

What is happening when a person runs from himself? He usually enters into a stage of anxiety in which there exists a feeling of "utter helplessness which pervades his being . . . his behavior is dictated by compulsiveness, so that he is driven rather than moved, and cannot feel that he is an active force in his own life . . . His relationship to himself is also impaired, involving both an extreme under-evaluation of his own actual assets and possibilities . . ." (Isidore Portney "The Anxiety States," *American Handbook of Psychiatry,* vol. I, p. 311)

When the Jew came out from Egypt was he really running from

himself or was he merely running from the physical miseries of bondage?

The Jew can ask himself the same question today. How well is he able to be at one with himself, undeterred by the pressures of indigence, undiverted by the ephemeral attractions of affluence?

16. Readiness for Prophecy

Leadership in Jewish life is associated with *charisma*. Charisma. means in Greek "endowed with grace." In modern sociological literature the term is to signify a specific type of authority and leadership.

Max Weber defines charisma as "a certain quality of an individual personality by virtue of which he is set apart from ordinary men and treated as endowed with supernatural, superhuman, or at least exceptional powers or qualities." (Max Weber, *The Theory of Social and Economic Organization*, 1947, pp. 358-392 and Reinhard Bendix, *Max Weber: An Intellectual Portrait*, 1960, ch. 10)

"The charismatic leader is perceived as a heroic, saintly or otherwise peculiarly gifted man whose authority is based upon those personal qualities. It is not just that he occupies high office but that he himself is specially deserving of respect and even adoration." (L. Broom and P. Selznick, *Sociology*, 1963 p. 678)

Jewish leaders such as prophets, kings, chiefs, and elders were attributed with charismatic qualities. About the prophets, the Talmud states, "The spirit of prophecy rests only upon persons who are (spiritually) wise, strong and wealthy." (*Talmud Sabbath* 92)

Upon seeing a king in Israel one must say, "Blessed be He who has imparted of His glory to them that fear Him." (*Talmud Berakot* 58a) Also, it has been indicated that every official position on earth was regarded as if by divine appointment and the rule of the king was compared with that of God.

As Rabbi Shila said, "Blessed be the All-Mighty who has made the earthly royalty on the model of the heavenly." (*Ibid*).

Furthermore, Maimonides states that "the first degree of prophecy consists in the divine assistance which is given to a person, and induces and encourages him to do something good or grand, i.e. to deliver a congregation of good men from the hands of evil doers, to

40

save one noble person, or to bring happiness to a large number of people . . .

"The degree of divine influence is called 'the spirit of the Lord,' and of the person who is under that influence is said that the spirit of the Lord *came upon him,* (i.e. 'And the spirit of the Lord came upon [Samson],' *Judges* 14:6) *clothed him,* (i.e. 'And the spirit of God clothed Gideon,' *Ibid.* 6:34); *or rested upon him,* (i.e. 'And it came to pass when the spirit rested upon (the *seventy* elders of Israel)' *Numbers* 11:25); or *the Lord was with him,* (i.e. 'And when the Lord raised up judges for them, and the Lord was with the judges . . .'" *Judges* 2:18).

"All the judges and noble chiefs of Israel possessed this first degree of prophecy, upon whom the Spirit of God rested." (See Maimonides, *Guide of the Perplexed,* Book 2, ch. 45)

Even in modern times the followers of Hasidic rabbis believe that their masters possess specific characteristics and personality; and that the rabbis are individuals endowed with supernatural powers or qualities.

Although the Spirit of God rested upon the leaders of Israel who were imbued with extraordinary physical and spiritual characteristics, nonetheless, the power of their strength, the intensity of their forcefulness, and even their endowment with the Spirit of God was only because of their association with the community.

The Spirit of God, or the super-human qualities of Jewish leaders are attributable to the Congregation of Israel.

Support for this argument can be found in the text which reads, "And the Lord spoke unto Moses, and Aaron in the land of Egypt, saying . . ." (*Exodus* 12:1)

Because the word "saying" is superfluous, Rabbi Akiba explains "saying" means that (God said to Moses) "go and tell the children of Israel (all that I say to you)." It was only for their sake that God spoke with Moses. For during all the *thirty-eight* years in which God was angry with Israel, He did not speak with Moses, as it is said, "So it came to pass, when all the men of war were consumed and dead from among the people, that the Lord spoke unto me . . ." (*Deuteronomy* 2:16-17)

This was not the case with Moses only, but with all prophets in Israel. Hence, Rabbi Simon ben Azzai adds, "I am not arguing against the words of my teacher, (Rabbi Akiba), but merely adding to his words. It was not with Moses alone that He spoke only be-

41

cause of Israel, but with all of the other prophets, likewise. He spoke only because of Israel . . ." (*Mekilta de Rabbi Ishmael* 1)

In fact, Maimonides states that "laws of nature demand that everyone should be a prophet, who has proper physical constitution and has been truly prepared through education and training." (Maimonides, *op. cit. Book* 2, ch. 32)

In Jewish life, therefore, everything and everyone must be in a stage of constant readiness for prophecy and holiness—a quality not exclusive to the leaders or the elite.

As the *Mekilta* states, "Before the land of Israel had been especially chosen, all lands were suitable for divine revelation; after the land of Israel had been chosen all other lands were eliminated.

"Before Jerusalem had been especially selected, the entire land of Israel was suitable for altars; after Jerusalem had been selected, all the rest of the land of Israel was eliminated . . .

"Before the Temple had been especially selected, the whole of Jerusalem was appropriate for the manifestation of the divine presence; after the Temple had been selected, the rest of Jerusalem was eliminated . . .

"Before Aaron had been especially chosen, all Israelites were qualified for the priesthood; after Aaron had been chosen, all other Israelites were eliminated.

"Before David had been chosen, all Israelites were eligible to kingship; after David had been chosen, all other Israelites were eliminated . . ." (*Ibid.*)

In Jewish life leadership emerges from and is sustained by the community. Although often times only one leader is chosen, everyone must qualify in order to serve if called upon.

17. Time Is for Free Men

And the Lord spoke unto Moses and Aaron in the land of Egypt, saying: 'This month shall be *unto you* the beginning of months; it shall be the first month of the year to you.' (Exodus 12:1-2)

What does this text mean? Certainly, it cannot mean that the first day of Nisan is the Jewish New Year because *Rosh Hashanah* is celebrated on the first day of Tishri. Can it be that in the Jewish calendar the New Year does not come in the first month? This is indeed the case. Perhaps some further elaboration is in order.

The calendar, or the system of reckoning time, is made with reference to some beginning. In Jewish life this beginning refers to the creation of the world. As "Rabbi Eliezer says: 'In Tishri the world was created'." (Talmud, Rosh Hashanah 10b.) Thus, the first day of Tishri is the Jewish New Year.

There could have been many other criteria for a beginning of reckoning time. For example, the birth of the patriarchs. But this too, is associated with Tishri. As the Talmud continues, "In Tishri the patriarchs (Abraham and Jacob) were born." (*Ibid.*)

The beginning of a family lineage or family system could have been another criteria for reckoning time. But this too, is associated with the month of Tishri. As the Talmud continues: "On New Year (the first day of Tishri) Sarah, Rachel and Hannah were remembered (to become mothers in Israel) . . ." (*Ibid*).

Still another criterion for reckoning of time could be the beginning of the formation of the Jews as a significant ethnic or national group. Joseph's release from prison was perhaps the beginning of Jewish concentration in Egypt. Or the point at which the Jews stopped the hard labor in Egypt could also be considered the beginning of Jewish nationhood. But both of these events took place in Tishri. As the Talmud says: "On New Year (the first day of Tishri) Joseph was discharged from prison; on New Year ceased the hard labor for our forefathers in Egypt." (*Ibid.*, 10b-11a)

There is, however, one phenomenon associated with Nisan and it is that "In Nisan (the children of Israel) were redeemed." (*Ibid.*) Thus the greatness of Nisan is that on that month the Jews were freed from slavery.

The greatest element in freedom is the element of *time*. A slave, as a property of and subject to another individual or state does not have "time." He, in his state of subjection, servitude and in compulsory service has no conception of time. To him it does not matter what time it is, what day it is, what month it is, or what year it is because his existence goes on aimlessly and timelessly without end, purpose or goal. Human beings' outlooks, goals and life perspectives are closely associated with time. Time provides basic human values, meaning and sequence. It provides the system which connects events to one another; it associates the past, the future and the present. It provides the succession to human experience which in fact gives all events human characteristics. From all these the slave is robbed. His life is not directed by time which gives meaning to his activities. He does not know the concept of duration, period, term, span, season, course, date, and year because his life is not related to time.

When the slave becomes free, the first thing that gives him self-perception as a human being is that he recognizes *time*. He recognizes that he is not owned or possessed by another, because by now he comprehends that time is his. He can do what he wants because he can freely utilize his time. This control and mastery of his own time, in fact, gives him independence and liberty. His time emancipates him, liberates him and provides him with a self-direction and self-reliance.

When the children of Israel were redeemed and liberated from Egypt, it was *TIME* with which they came first in contact. The conceptualization of time gave them the meaning of freedom, gave them the direction of self-government. This realization of time came to the Jews on the month of Nisan. Therefore, any event that has to do with time or season, should be associated with Nisan, the month of liberation and recognition of time. This is actually suggested in the text: "This month shall be *unto you*, the beginning of months." *To you*, specifically this has a more significant meaning. When the Jew reckons time, when he considers the months, the years, the seasons, it should be associated with that month which was the birth, the beginning of conception of time.

Nachmanides states that the names of the Hebrew months were adopted in Babylonia. (Exodus 12:2) Initially Jewish months did not have any names. They were called first month, second month, etc. For example, the Jewish New Year is described as:

> ... in the seventh month, of the first day of the month, ye shall have a holy convocation ... it is a day of blowing the shofar ... (Numbers 29:1)

Yom Kippur is described as:
> ... on the tenth day of the seventh month is the day of atonement ... (Leviticus 23:27)

Succoth is described as:
> On the fifteenth day of this seventh month is the feast of tabernacles. (*Ibid.* 23:24)

Passover, however, falls on the first month—on the month when the concept of time actualized in the minds of the Jews when they

44

became free. All other seasons and holidays, thus should be associated with the outcoming from Egypt.

And ever since that time of their liberation, great events, tragic moments, beautiful seasons, and diversified periods crown and signify Jewish history.

18. 'I Commanded the Sea to Divide'

Through many negotiations and wonders, Pharaoh let the children of Israel leave Egypt, the land of slavery. As the Israelites were moving toward the wilderness, Pharaoh regretted letting them go. He took 600 chosen chariots . . . and pursued the children of Israel.

When Pharaoh and his army drew near, the Israelites lifted up their eyes and saw the Egyptians marching after them. They were frightened as they noted that they were surrounded on three sides.

The sea was blocking them in the front, the enemy was pursuing from the back, and the wild beasts of the wilderness, trying to attack them from the side. (*Midrash Rabbah Exodus* 21:5)

They raised their eyes to their Heavenly Father and cried unto God . . . Moses, too, prayed. And the Lord said to him, "Why do you cry to Me, speak to the children of Israel to move forward! Lift up your rod and stretch out your hand over the sea and divide it . . . And the children of Israel went into the middle of the sea upon dry ground, and the waters were a wall unto them on their right hand and on their left . . ." (*Exodus* 14:15-22)

Much has been said about the dividing and the crossing of the Red Sea. With the great emphasis placed upon science as a systematized knowledge based on observation and verification, the event of exodus has been interpreted and given understanding within a framework of scientific probabilities.

Judaism as a theological system cannot conceive of the dividing and the crossing of the Red Sea purely as an event that is scientifically plausible. For Israel this event was not simply a source of a verified, objective, historic occurrence.

This event represented the actual foundation of Israel's existence as the people of God. For Israel this was an event of *revelation, faith,* and the *acknowledgement of God.* It was the event where

45

"Israel saw the great work which the Lord did . . . the people feared the Lord, and they believed in the Lord . . ." (*Ibid.* 14:31)

Those philosophers who believe that God does not change nature's course give a scientifically sound explanation to the great and miraculous events. But again, it must be pointed out that theological systems are based on people's trust, faith, and unshakable belief in God, and not on scientific probabilities.

This concern of changing the course of nature and the reaffirmation of faith is even apparent in the rabbinic literature. The Midrash states, "When God said to Moses 'Lift up your rod and stretch out your hand over the sea . . .' Moses said to the Holy One, blessed be He, 'How can You command me to divide the sea and convert it to dry land . . . Did you not promise that the sea would not be changed into dry land . . . ?' "

"God replied . . . 'It was I Who made a condition at the very beginning (when creating the sea) that I would one day divide it . . .'

"After hearing this, Moses immediately obeyed God's command and went to divide the sea, but the sea refused to comply . . .

"Moses went to report to God, 'The sea refuses to be divided,' What did God do? He placed His right hand upon the right hand of Moses . . . thereupon as soon as Moses raised his hand over the sea, it divided itself . . ." (*Midrash Rabbah Exodus* 21:6)

Thus, according to the rabbis, miracles such as dividing the sea are not an act by which the course of nature is being changed. In fact, the rabbis state that . . . the miracles are to some extent also natural; for they say, when God created the universe with its present physical properties, He made it part of these properties, that they should produce certain miracles at certain times . . . But the thing itself was affected according to the fixed laws of nature . . . e.g. that God gave the waters the property of joining together, and of flowing in a downward direction, and of separating only at the time when the Egyptians were drowned, and in a particular place . . . (Maimonides, *Guide of the Perplexed* Book 2, chap. 29)

This again is supported by the Midrash.

"And God said, 'Let the waters under heaven be gathered together unto one place, and let the dry land appear.' (*Genesis* 1:9) Rabbi Johanan said, 'The Holy One, blessed be He, made a stipulation with the sea that it should divide before Israel . . .'

"Rabbi Jeremiah ben Eleazar said, 'Not with the sea alone did God make a stipulation, but with everything which was in the six days of creation ... I commanded the sea to divide, and the heavens to be silent before Moses ... I commanded the sun and the moon to stand still before Joshua; I commanded the ravens to feed Elijah, I commanded the fire to do no harm to Hananiah, Mishael and Azariah; I commanded the lions not to harm Daniel; the heavens to open before Ezekiel; the fish to vomit forth Jonah." (*Midrash Rabbah Genesis* 5:5)

Hence the event of the exodus was the principal event when God revealed Himself to the entire Congregation of Israel. It was that event when the Jews also demonstrated their complete and perfect faith in God.

As the Midrash states, "The sea was divided only after Israel had stepped into it and the waters had reached their noses, only then did it become dry land." (*Midrash Rabbah Exodus* 21:10)

Furthermore, the Israelites "did not say to Moses, 'How can we go out into the desert without having provisions for the journey?' But they believed in Moses and followed him . . ." (*Mekilta de Rabbi Ishmael,* Tractate Beshalach chap. 4)

19. Should the Jew Claim Selection?

Each group considers its way of life the natural and the best way. Strong identification with the familiar and the devaluation of the foreign is called *ethnocentrism.*

It is the feeling that one's own culture is the best in all respects and that others are in varying degrees inferior, barbaric, heathen or outlandish. (L. Broom and P. Selznick, *Sociology,* p. 57).

Ethnocentrism is a feeling of superiority toward the ingroup and inferiority towards the outgroup. Extreme ethnocentrism leads to unnecessary objection to the richness and knowledge of other cultures.

Although ethnocentrism impedes the sharing of ideas and skills that might bring a society closer to its own goals, nonetheless, it is essential in every society in order to develop a feeling of group loyalty, cohesion and a drive for continuity.

There is deep concern in America about assimilation and the lack of identification with Jewishness. Young people today feel uncomfortable being ethnocentric about Judaism and things associated with Jews.

A Jewish college student writes, "I am a Jew by birth, but not a very good Jew at that, if I am to be judged by the standards prescribed in the Torah and the Talmud. My concept of the nature of divinity is not completely in accordance with that which a Jew should maintain.

"I agree that God's power is extensive, and that He Himself is responsible for everything that exists, but I am inclined to disbelief that he holds special favors toward Jews.

"To me He is a Universal Spirit, no matter by what Name He may be called, Who has always existed and will continue to exist forever. All the people in the history of the world lived under His reign; I cannot accept the fact that He has chosen the Jews as benefactors of His immortal kindness—that the Jews are chosen people . . ."

Throughout the ages there were many who apologized constantly, for Jewish ethnocentric statements, attitudes and sentiments. There are many today, particularly among the young people, who still feel uncomfortable that Jews claim some sort of superiority over others.

It should be recognized, however, that this trait is not exclusively associated with Jews. Some sort of feeling of superiority (*ethnocentrism*) exists among all peoples and nations. It is this feeling of superiority that gives meaning and significance for group survival.

If Jewish youth is filled with humility let it be on a personal basis. On a group level, he must find some cause for pride.

God gave the Torah and the Ten Commandments to the children of Israel. The Ten Commandments open, "I am the Lord your God Who brought you out of the land of Egypt . . ." God did not say, "I am the Lord your God Who created the world . . ." or, "Who made the heaven and the earth . . ." but, "I am the Lord your God Who brought you out of the land of Egypt, out of the house of bondage."

It was at this time—when the Jews came out from Egypt and received the Torah—that God glorified and magnified Himself and became known throughout the world.

God said to the Children of Israel, "You have seen what I did unto the Egyptians and how I bore you on eagle's wings and brought you to Me. Now if you will obey Me faithfully and keep My covenant, you shall be My treasured possession among all the peoples. Indeed all the earth is Mine, but you shall be to Me a kingdom of priests and a holy nation." (*Exodus* 19:4-6).

It was the entire group that had the privilege actually to see and hear the great revelation. The Torah was *not* given to Adam, the first man, *nor* was it given to Noah, the survivor of the Flood. The Torah was *not* given to Abraham, the patriarch, *nor* was it given to Jacob the father of the 12 Tribes.

The Torah *was* given to the Children of Israel, to the entire group and not to selected individuals.

The Torah was *not* given in the land of Israel, but in the wilderness, in the open before all the people of Israel. As the *Mekilta* states, "Why was the Torah not given in the land of Israel? In order that the nations of the world should not have the excuse for saying, 'Because it was given in Israel's land therefore we have not accepted it.'

"Another reason was to avoid causing dissension among the tribes. Else one tribe might have said, 'In my territory was the Torah given . . .' therefore, the Torah was given in the desert, publicly and openly, in a place belonging to no one." (*Mekilta de Rabbi Ishmael,* Tractate Bechodesh, chap. 5).

The Torah was *not* given in secret in a "still small voice," but "there was thunder and lightning, . . . and a very loud blast of the horn . . ." for everyone to hear.

This group of people has been selected to receive the words of God with all its glory and often tragic consequences. As God said, "It (was) not because (they were) the most numerous of peoples that the Lord set His heart on (them) and chose (them)—indeed, (they) are the smallest of peoples, but it was because the Lord loved (them) and kept the oath He made to (their) fathers . . ." (*Deuteronomy* 7:7-8)

There were many times the Jews did not meet their obligations and shunned their Jewishness. And there was many a time that the hands of the Lord were heavy upon them. But are the Jews to claim a specific kind of selection only when they fail to meet their responsibility?

Are they only chosen when there is a requirement for sacrifice? Can they not also claim selection for honor? Should they have no feeling of ethnocentrism with which to justify their existence in a hostile world?

20. The Hebrew Slave

Human servitude was always closely associated with economic considerations. Even in the United States during slavery, the value of slaves fluctuated with the price of cotton.

When the price of cotton rose, the value of slaves doubled, "and with every increase in value the difficulty of breaking the status of Negro slavery increased." (Charles S. Johnson, "Race Relations and Social Change," in Edgar T. Thomson [ed.] *Race Relations and Race Problem*, 1939, p. 282.)

In the 1800's, when the price of cotton rose, the belief in slavery, which had been on the decline for a century, began to revive in the South. After 1830, an extensive literature attempted to justify slavery and showed that slavery was not contrary to nature, nor to religion.

As George Fitzhugh, in 1854, said, "Our Southern patriots, at the time of the Revolution, finding Negroes expensive and useless, became warm anti-slavery men. We, their sons, having learned to make cotton and sugar, find slavery very useful and profitable. . .

"We have almost all human and divine authority on our side of the argument. The Bible nowhere condemns and throughout recognizes slavery." (Quoted in George E. Simpson and J. Milton Yinger, *Racial and Cultural Minorities*, 1958, p. 124.)

In the Torah the Ten Commandments are followed by the Jewish civil law, such as indemnification for injuries done to a fellow man and duties toward persons who have no legal claims.

It is interesting to note that Jewish civil law opens with the Hebrew slave. The Torah reads, "When you acquire a Hebrew slave, he shall serve six years; in the seventh year he shall be freed, without payment. . . (*Exodus* 21:2).

In ancient days there were two ways a Hebrew could become a slave:

1) A person whom the court sold without his consent for theft. The court had the jurisdiction to sell a person who was caught stealing and had no money to pay.

As it is written, "(If one was caught stealing) he shall make restitution; if he lacks the means, he shall be sold for his theft." (*Ibid.* 22:2).

2) A person who willingly sold himself because of extreme pov-

erty. As it is written, "If your brother, among you, in grave poverty sells himself to you . . ." (*Leviticus* 25:39).

The Hebrew slave during his servitude had to be treated as a hired laborer. His master had to place him on an equal basis with himself in meat and drink, in lodging and in bedclothes, and had to behave toward him in a brotherly manner.

The master could not use him in a derogatory service, "not even letting him carry his garments after him to the bath house." (*Yad*, Abadim; *Shulchan Aruch, Yoreh Deah* 267). As a matter of fact the Talmud declares, "Whoever buys a Hebrew slave buys a master for himself." (*Talmud Kiddushin* 20a.)

After serving six years the slave is free to go. But if he does not want to take advantage of this privilege, instead, he declares, "I love my master . . . I do not wish to be freed." His master shall take him before the judges. He shall be brought to the door or the doorpost, and his master shall pierce his ear with an awl; and he shall then remain his slave for life." (*Exodus* 21:5-6).

The reason why the ear was pierced and no other organ is explained in the Talmud.

"Rabban Johanan Ben Zakkai used to expound this verse . . . 'Why was the ear singled out from all the other limbs of the body? The Holy One, blessed be He, said, "This ear which heard My voice on Mount Sinai when I proclaimed, 'For unto Me the children of Israel are servants, they are My servants and not servants of servants.' And yet this man went and acquired a master for himself —let it be bored." (*Talmud Kiddushin* 22b).

Accordingly, his ear should have been pierced as soon as he became a slave, not after six years. But before he became an actual slave, he could not know the full meaning of slavery. Only after he has been exposed to this low social position and became subservient to a master could he appreciate his freedom.

But if he chose to remain a slave and thereby refused to assume the responsibility of life, despite this personal humility, his ear had to be pierced because he had had the chance to go free.

The reason why the piercing was done at the door or the doorpost is also explained in the Talmud.

"Rabbi Simeon Ben Rabbi (Judah the Prince) too expounded this verse . . . 'Why were the door and the doorpost singled out from all other parts of the house?' The Holy One, blessed be He, said, 'The door and the doorpost which were witnesses in Egypt when I passed over the lintel and the doorposts and proclaimed, 'For unto Me the children of Israel are servants, they are My servants and not servants of servants, so I brought them forth from bondage to freedom,' yet this man went and acquired a master for himself—let him be bored in their (door and doorpost) presence'." . . . (*Ibid.*)

Again, the door symbolizes this man's freedom. He could have walked through this door as a free man but he did not take advantage of this opportunity, he chose to serve his master. So, the piercing was done at the door.

According to Maimonides, piercing of the ear was done only on a slave that was sold by the court without his consent. A person that sold himself could not extend the period of his servitude by having his right ear pierced.

Conditions that brought a man to sell himself because of extreme poverty were indeed a community responsibility as well. The community should have assumed responsibility and aided the person in so great a poverty that the only course left was to sell himself into slavery.

How could a Jewish community stand by and observe that one of its members must sell himself into servitude because of extreme poverty? At no time could the value of a man—his service and integrity—be measured by the price of cotton.

21. A New Religious Art?

Much has been said about the lack of the development of Jewish art. Most of the comments and speculations are related to a Biblical prohibition as is indicated by the statement of Immanuel Benzinger: "It was the religion of the Jew that precluded the full development of the art of sculpture . . . In the most ancient times when images were not proscribed, the technical ability to make them artistically was lacking; and when in later periods this artistic skill might have been acquired from others, images were forbidden.

"The persistent fight of the prophets against images was waged with such success that in the end not only was any representation of the deity forbidden, but even the portraiture of living beings in general, man or beast."

The preclusion of fuller development of Jewish art is associated with the following Biblical prohibition:

> Thou shalt not make unto thee a graven image, nor any manner of likeness, of any thing that is in heaven above, or that is in the earth beneath, or that is in the water under the earth; thou shalt not bow down unto them, nor serve them. (*Exodus* 20:4-5)

Obviously this could not have had such an impact on Jews were it not for the fact that artistic expressions were associated with religions. This thought, however, needs further analysis.

One of the most important aspects in Jewish life has been the dichotomy of the *Kodesh,* or the sacred and the *Chol,* or the secular or profane. A religion that prescribes and specifically defines almost all aspects of the sacred and profane had to devise a system by which these two opposing phenomena could independently emerge and expand. Thus, it prohibited the sacred to be profaned and allowed the secular to be made holy. In Jewish theology the emphasis is on making the secular sacred. *Shechita,* ritual slaughter, is an example. The animal has to be ritually prepared so that the secular should have a religious significance. A person may enjoy much of the secular and the worldly in life if he pronounces a blessing with God's name to transform the secular into sacred.

The sacred, however, was never made into secular. For example, all things pertaining to Temple service had to remain for all time in sacred status and could never assume the role of secular. Even the priest was a sacred object. So when the priest's daughter engages in immoral activities she defiles her father, the priest. (*Leviticus* 21:9)

Most art objects, particularly with the Jew, were associated with the sacred. Religion did not allow one to deviate from the sacred. The group under such system did not have the freedom to grow and develop further artistic designs because it had to maintain all that which was prescribed and associated with sacred things.

This is clearly indicated in the text, "The Lord spoke to Moses, saying: Tell the Israelite people to bring Me gifts . . . and let them make Me a sanctuary that I may dwell among them. Exactly as I show you—the pattern of the tabernacle and the pattern of all its furnishings—so shall you make it." (*Exodus* 25:1-9)

The Rashbam explains that God showed Moses a model of the tabernacle and the vessels and all had to be done in accordance with that display. It seems that a system with this strong prescription of artistic objects lent little freedom to the development of the arts.

Even the making of the candlestick is fully detailed, describing its base, its shaft, its cups, its knobs, and its flowers—still the Bible specifically states:

> And see that thou make them after their pattern, which is being shown thee in the mount. (*Exodus* 25:40)

A strict dividing line between the sacred and the secular has shown manifestation in other areas of Jewish life. For example, the Hebrew language assumed for a long period of time among Jews the role of *Lashon Kodesh,* the holy language, used only in connection with the sacred. It was necessary to utilize another language for the secular. Even to this very day there are groups who ascribe this very role to Hebrew.

Thus, throughout the ages, virtually all artistic expressions were associated with religion. Furthermore, one had to become imbued with deep, inner emotions and religiosity to express the sacred through art. Although the Jew had the inner emotional and religious qualities, he did not develop art because he did not dare to relate it to the sacred. Today when he dares to relate art to the sacred, he should also cultivate the inner emotional involvement through which art emerges. A new phase of Jewish religious art may result.

22. Family Ties and the Golden Calf

The Bible gives a detailed description of the episode of the Golden Calf. The text reads in part: "And when the people saw that Moses delayed to come down from the mount, the people gathered themselves together unto Aaron, and said unto him: 'Up, make us a God who shall go before us . . .' and all the people broke off the golden rings which were in their ears, and brought them unto Aaron. And he received it at their hand, and fashioned it with a graving tool, and made it a molten calf; and they said: 'This is thy god, O Israel, which brought thee up out of the land of Egypt' . . . And the Lord spoke unto Moses: '. . . thy people . . . have turned aside quickly out of the way which I commanded them . . . Now therefore let Me alone, that My wrath may wax hot against them, and that I may consume them' . . . And Moses pleaded before God, and said: '. . . Turn from Thy fierce wrath and repent this evil against Thy people. Remember Abraham, Isaac and Israel, Thy servants . . .' " (*Exodus* 32:1-13)

Elsewhere the Torah gives a detailed description about a special ritual involving a red cow, an observance relevant to becoming ritually clean.* The text reads, "The Lord spoke to Moses and Aaron saying: Instruct the Israelite people to bring you a red cow without blemish, in which there is no defect and on which no yoke has been laid . . . the cow shall be burned . . . a man who is clean shall gather up the ashes . . . and deposit them outside the camp in a clean place, to be kept for water of lustration for the Israelite community. It is for cleansing." (*Numbers* 19:1-9)

Rashi, the great commentator finds a relationship between the Golden Calf and the Red Cow. He states,

> This may be likened to the son of a maidservant who soiled the palace of the king, they said: 'let his mother come and clean up.' Similarly let the heifer come and make atonement for the (golden) calf.

To understand this comment by Rashi it is helpful to consider two of the basic factors that have contributed to Jewish continuity. These are:

1) The family system and
2) a strong association with the past.

Throughout history Jews have placed a high value upon family life. For example, they despised the bachelor, and pitied the spinster; only he who founded a house in Israel was worthy to be considered a full-fledged member of the community, only she who had become a mother in Israel had realized her destiny. (Israel Cohen, *Jewish Life in Modern Times*, p. 40). Furthermore, Jewish tradition stressed chastity, matrimonial fidelity, desire for large families, respect of children for their parents, unlimited love and devotion of parents for their children, women not entering public life, daughters remain-

---

* Preceding Passover, proper steps to become ritually clean had to be taken as preparation for the eating of the Paschal lamb. The reading of the text of the red cow in the synagogues as a special ritual has been prescribed. Hence the Sabbath is called *Sabbath Parah*, named after this ritual text.

ing at home until marriage, husband's authority . . . (Arthur Ruppin, *The Jews in the Modern World*, p. 277).

Strong association with the past is exemplified by the zealous observance of the religious patterns associated with the departed. For example, if one would ask what area of religion has found the greatest expression in America, without hesitation, the answer would be observances related to the memory of the dead.

This is manifested in the yearly visitation to the cemeteries before the high holidays and the increase of synagogue attendance at *Yiskor*, memorial services. Disproportionate observance of the *Yahrzeit*, the anniversary of death, to other religious services; the saying of the *kaddish* in relative magnitude to any other prayers similarly are manifestations of the same thinking.

Furthermore, activities such as dedicating memorials, tablets, lamps, donations in memory of . . . all are indications of an attitude of maintaining a strong association with the past. This great attachment with those religious practices which are associated with the passing from life are in essence contributing factors to the perpetuity of the Jew.

Now these two principal factors, the family and association with the past which help maintain Jewish continuity, are not only part of the Jews' social life but are actually imbedded into the Jewish theological frame of reference. When seeking explanation to the red heifer (which according to some authorities is a ceremony with no rational basis) one must reach out into an area which has been part of Jewish life. An explanation that the red heifer is to be viewed as the mother who must come and make atonement for her daughter, the golden calf, is possible and meaningful only in a religious system in which the family plays such a role and in which a mother feels impelled to assume responsibility and can make atonement for her child.

The strong association with the past also as a characteristic of the Jew consequently contributes to continuity. When Moses was praying for forgiveness, he asked that Abraham, Isaac, and Israel be remembered. Moses actually asked that the forefathers' virtues may shield Israel and that their circumstances and life episodes be considered as that of the contemporary Jew. This strong association with the past was the main object in Moses' prayer: "Remember Abraham, Isaac and Israel . . ."

But there are greater ties, than just the mere fact of descent, between the contemporary Jew and his past. He strongly desires that the past and the present merge to comprise the wholeness of Jewish existence. Thus the Midrash adds:

"Moses argued: 'If it is burning that they (the Jews) deserve (for worshipping the calf) then remember (O Lord) Abraham, who jeopardized his life in the fiery furnace in order to be burnt for Thy name (Midrash Rabba, Genesis 38:3) and let his burning cancel the burning of his children; and if it is decapitation that they deserve, then remember their father Isaac who stretched forth his neck on the altar ready to be slaughtered for Thy name, and let now his immolation cancel the immolation of his children; and if it is banishment that they deserve then remember their father Jacob who was banished from his father's house to Haran. Let all those acts of (the patriarchs) now atone for their act (of sin in worshipping the calf).' This is why (Moses) said: Remember Abraham, Isaac and Israel . . ." (Midrash Rabba, Exodus)

American society has provided much opportunity for the Jew to become incorporated into the larger social system. Consequently, as Jewish life, in this dynamic society loses some of the many other binding characteristics, there will be a need for greater reliance upon forces such as the *strong family system* and the values attached to *strong association with the past.*

23. No One Need Be Ashamed

Social and personal adjustments that Jews make in the American society have taken on different forms. Whereas some persistently continued the traditional Jewish life pattern, others have adopted an entirely new way of life totally removed from Judaism.

Not all individuals, however, fall into these two extreme categories. Most American Jews function between these two opposite poles. Jewish adjustment processes, by and large, are ordered into the following continuum:

1. Traditional—Those who did not try to remove themselves from the Jewish community life but continued, more or less, with a traditional pattern based on Jewish values. Most people in this category are comfortable about their Jewishness and take great pride in all Jewish accomplishments.

2. Transitional—Those who tried and are still trying to remove themselves from Jewish life patterns, but were not able to make a successful transition, whether because (a) they met with external resistance, or (b) they were deeply involved psychologically and emotionally in their being Jewish.

3. Translocational—Those who were able to acculturate to the extent that they relinquished their language, customs, food habits and expectations of Jewish life and substituted items from the larger cultural milieu.

Among these groups there are many who have fully reconciled themselves to their new life patterns. Also, there are many who still continue to rebel and express a dissatisfaction about Jews and Judaism. Some even developed a self-hatred and a negative chauvinism with a deeply-seated feeling of unworthiness, inferiority and blame.

This lack of confidence and this pessimistic attitude and dismay is not only characteristic of modern times. Even in the time of Moses, despite the great wonders and miracles, there were those who became terrified and awe-stricken at every crisis and discomfort.

At the sea, as the Egyptians pursued, the frightened Israelites said to Moses, "Because there were no graves in Egypt, that you have taken us away to die in the wilderness? What have you done to us in bringing us out of Egypt?" (*Exodus* 14:11)

At Marah, because of the water crisis, the pessimistic people murmured against Moses saying, "What shall we drink?" (*Ibid.* 15:24)

At the wilderness of Sin, because of another water crisis, the discouraged people quarreled with Moses, ". . . Why did you bring us up from Egypt, to kill us and our children and livestock with thirst?" (*Ibid.* 17:2-3)

At Mount Sinai, because of impatience, the distrusting people gathered against Aaron and said to him, "Come, make us a god who shall go before us, for that man Moses, who brought us from the land of Egypt—we cannot tell what has happened to him." (*Ibid.* 32:1)

These voices were signs of dissatisfaction and distrust. These were the voices of the alarmists, scare-mongers and petrified Israelites who did not have the strong dedication and devotion to the group and its purposes.

What creates this unhealthy distrust and pessimism within the Jewish community?

It is necessary to point out that wherever deeply seated feelings of unworthiness emerge within Judaism, it is usually because there are serious defects in the community cohesiveness. It is not merely a problem concerning certain individuals. The Jewish community has failed to provide a proper *esprit de corps* that would give rise to a more positive attitude and enthusiastic devotion to the group and its values.

"Moses assembled all the congregation of the children of Israel . . ." (*Ibid.* 35:1) It is interesting to note that at no other place until now, is it mentioned in the Torah that *Moses assembled all the children of Israel.*

In Egypt, the Torah states, "Moses and Aaron went and gathered all the elders of the children of Israel." (*Ibid.* 4:29) At the preparation for Passover, before the Exodus, the Torah states, "Moses called all the elders of Israel . . ." (*Ibid.* 12:21) At Mount Sinai the Torah states, "Moses brought the people out of the camp to meet God . . ." (*Ibid.* 19:17)

The assemblage of the entire congregation of Israel was not commanded in Egypt, neither, at the performance of the rituals, nor at the giving of the Torah, but only after the great events had taken place.

It was an assemblage that was in addition to the great events. Perhaps this was to indicate that the Jews' common bondage of the past, their common observance of Passover, their common witnessing of the great revelation were not enough to establish the needed *esprit de corps*. Because during these events voices of dissatisfaction and rebellion were still heard in the camp of Israel.

It was necessary therefore, in addition to the common heritage, to establish assemblies in which every Jew could participate; congregations of which every Jew could feel an important part.

Such communities, based on unity and solidarity, in turn could provide the necessary enthusiasm and dedication for all its members so that no one need be ashamed.

59

III. From
THE BOOK OF LEVITICUS

24. Rare Privilege—With Obligations

The third book of the Torah in Hebrew is called *Vayikra*, literally "and (the Lord) called" after the first word of the text. In English it is called Leviticus derived from the Latin and originally from the Greek. Formerly the book was known as *Torat Kohanim*, "The Priestly Code" because it is composed mainly of laws relating to Temple rituals, sacrifices and sacred performances of the priests and Levites.

The text reads:

> *VAYIKRA*—And the Lord called unto Moses, and spoke unto him out of the tent of the meeting . . . (Leviticus 1:1)

Nachmanides notes that in no other place is this expression—the Lord called—used with respect to Moses and explains its use in this verse as follows:

> Moses was not able to enter into the tent of meeting, because the cloud abode thereon and the glory of the Lord filled the tabernacle (Exodus 40:35)

Therefore Moses needed a special call or invitation to enter.

The Midrash comments on the text "And the Lord called unto Moses . . ." saying: "What is the authoritative basis for the following statement: 'A scholar who lacks common sense, a carcass is better than he.'? You have adequate proof that this is so. Go forth and learn from Moses, the father of wisdom, the father of the prophets, who brought Israel out of Egypt, through whom so many miracles were performed in Egypt, and awesome acts at the Red Sea, who ascended to the heavens above, and brought down the Torah from heaven, and occupied himself with the making of the Tabernacle, and yet entered not the innermost part of the Sanctuary until God called him, as it is said, And the Lord called unto Moses . . ." (*Midrash Rabba,* Vayikra 15)

This Midrash helps us understand the role of the religious

63

scholar in Jewish life. It was a role with rare privileges and unusual obligations. Traditionally the *Talmid Hacham,* the learned man, enjoyed the greatest honor in Jewish life. Jewish law exempted him from the payment of taxes and from performing specific public duties. (*Schulchan Aruch, Yorei Deah* 243). He was sought for the most eligible daughters of the Jewish community. He and his colleagues formed the Jewish upper class and the aristocracy. Even the Jewish mothers' lullabies were full of dreams expressing the hope that their children become *talmidei hachamim,* Torah scholars.

The high value placed upon learning is illustrated in the Mishnah: "A scholar, even if he be an illegitimate child, takes precedence over an ignorant high priest." (*Talmud, Horayot* 13a) Because learning was so highly valued among Jews, even today there is still some awe associated with the learned man.

In addition to the privileges the learned man enjoyed, he had an added measure of duties and responsibilities. One of his major duties was to maintain the image of the *Talmid Hacham.* He had to behave in a way that was becoming of a learned man.

Breach of these high standards was considered a most serious offense. Maimonides states that if learned men do not behave in the way expected of them, they commit a *Chilul Hashem,* or, desecrate the Divine Name. The Rambam goes on saying, "there are many other ways (in addition to the ones that have been enumerated) through which one may desecrate the Divine Name. One of these is when a great man in Torah learning (or a man) well known for his religious piety does something by which he elicits unpleasant comments. Although these acts are not necessarily prohibited by Jewish law, because they are not becoming for a learned man, they are considered *Chilul Hashem,* desecration of the Divine Name." (*Yod,* Yesodei Torah 11)

It is a communal responsibility to uplift the honor and respect of the Torah scholar. But it is equally important that Torah scholars maintain their dignity and reaffirm the image of the Torah scholar through their own exemplary behavior.

25. Cultures in Conflict

Culture conflict arises where individuals, groups or societies are in conflict with one another over opposing cultural values. Sabbath observance among Jews is a good example of a clash in values currently being debated in various governmental circles. A Jew who strictly observes the Sabbath and adheres to an important cultural-religious value on the one hand may also be forced to observe Sunday, the day of rest in American society. Such a religious man cannot desecrate the Sabbath nor can he continue his secular activities on Sunday, a prohibition based on a conflicting principle.

The important thing is that culture conflict comes about when there are two conflicting ideologies, that is when people adhere to principles which are in opposition. Thus, culture conflict can arise only when principle is involved. If there is no principle, or if people do not adhere to their ideologies, or if those concepts that once mattered now make no difference, one ideology becomes engulfed or submerged into the other and the conflict ceases.

Assimilation is actually a process by which social or religious values either diminish or submerge into other ideologies. Once dissident values become subordinated into a stronger, or more desirable system, there will be no more culture conflict, for there will be no conflict.

Consequently, individuals identifying themselves with a cultural heritage through specific ideologies slowly lose this identification should a new or different ideology take predominance. This period of transition, when the person moves away from observance of the strict code of behavior and adopts the new, is a difficult one. For example, with the immigrant this transitional period presents a state of personal disorganization. As W. I. Thomas states: "The decay of traditional social organization is . . . due to the appearance and development of new attitudes leading to activities which do not comply with the socially recognized and sanctioned schemes of behavior." (W. I. Thomas and Florian Znaniecki, *The Polish Peasant in Europe and America,* Vol. 11, p. 1303) It is only painful during the period of transition. However, once individuals are over the hurdle there are no more culture conflicts.

The text deals with dietary prescriptions. The Torah enumerates the type of animals that are permitted and those that are prohibited. The text reads:

And the Lord spoke unto Moses and Aaron saying unto them: "Speak unto the children of Israel, saying: These are the living things which ye may eat among all the beasts that are on the earth" . . . (Leviticus 11:1-2) To this the Midrash adds:

R. Tanhum b. Hanilai said: "This may be compared with the case of a physician who went to visit two sick persons. To one who (he judged) would live, he said: 'This you may eat, that you may not eat.' But, concerning the one who was to die, he said: 'Give him whatever he asks.' Thus, of those whose orientation is not toward the life of the World to Come, it is written, Every moving thing that liveth shall be for food for you; as the green herb have I given you all (Genesis 9:3). But to those who are destined for the life of the World to Come (He said) these are the living things which ye may not eat . . ."

The person who keeps his ideology alive in a society that provides other standards and values has limitations and conflicts. This inevitably presents a "culture conflict" because of communal values which oppose the standards to which he adheres. There is always the temptation to assimilate if the individual develops new attitudes to the extent that he is willing to drop his cultural heritage, and dietary prohibitions may be one of the things to be dropped, he may find a temporary personal disorganization, but not a cultural conflict. Such a person will have no limitations in his behavior because the formal ideology will vanish from existence. But that Jew who maintains his religious values has become fully aware of the culture conflict that exists in the society of which he has become a part. And to this type of culture conflict the Jew continually tries to make adequate adjustments with a most impressive measure of success.

26. The Evil Power of Talk

The Torah deals with the laws concerning the leper, as it is written, "The Lord spoke unto Moses, saying: This shall be the law of the leper . . ." (Leviticus 14:1 ff) The rabbis associate the leper with "evil tongue," with gossiping, indicating that the punishment for gossip is leprosy.

Two types of gossiping can be recognized in the interacting processes of the community. One is gossip as a form of social control. Every community in addition to its written laws, has traditions, customs and mores which cannot be enforced by its law enforcing agents and agencies, but only through community pressure and control. One of these forms of control is gossip. The deviants and the non-conformists are talked against and criticized which keeps them in line. Although the gossipers are not aware that they are exercising a specific social and community function with their gossip, nevertheless they are contributing to the maintenance of community norms.

The second type of gossip is *Lashon Horah,* or "evil tongue." This form of gossip carries with it a deeply seated maliciousness. It moves into the private affairs of others and intends to destroy the individuals involved. It is specifically prohibited in the Torah, as it is written: Thou shalt not go up and down as a talebearer among thy people. (Leviticus 19:16)

It must be recognized that whereas the first form of gossip performs a community function, that of social control, it is still considered morally and ethically wrong in Jewish life. The second form, however, is actually abhorred and hated by God. As the Midrash relates: the rabbis said: . . . there are seven things that are hated and abhorred by God, of which the seventh one is the worst of all: 1) haughty eyes; 2) lying tongue; 3) hands that shed innocent blood; 4) a heart that deviseth wicked thoughts; 5) feet that are swift in running to evil; 6) a false witness that breatheth out lies; 7) he that soweth discord among brethren. (Midrash, Leviticus 16:1)

Judaism as a theological system is extremely concerned about those aspects of life which can do damage to individuals, such as gossip and malicious talk against one's neighbor, because they are very difficult to stop or control. The Talmudic literature is full of strong warnings against evil talk. For example: "One of the four groups that will not conceive the presence of God is the one that talks evil." (Talmud, Sotah 42a) "Of one who speaks evil God says 'I and he cannot live together in the world'." (Talmud, Erachin 15) "All those that speak evil tongue force the presence of God away from earth to heaven" (Midrash, Deuteronomy 5).

Moses Ben Hayyim Alshekh (c. 1507-c. 1600) asked: "If evil talk is such a grave offense in Jewish life and if individuals are punished by leprosy, how come that there are so few lepers around these days? Is it possible that evil tongue has ceased among Jews?" He answers that it is precisely because the air is so full of evil talk that the punishment had to be mitigated. Should leprosy still be the punishment for gossip, most of us would be covered from head to toe with leprosy. (B. Yeushson, *Fun Unser Alt'n Oitzer*, vol. 3, p. 83)

Perhaps Jewish communities need to give serious consideration to the negative aspects and the unfortunate consequences of *Lashon Horah*. According to another Midrash, even Moses was concerned about it. As it was stated: Moses was wondering if the great sin of the Jews was the cause of their being in bondage, even worse than other nations. But when he recognized that there is evil tongue among them, he changed his question and asked: How can they be redeemed? (Midrash, Exodus 1) As Jewish communities need greater unification in their efforts and purposes, gossip can only have a deteriorating effect on all the great potential that could be proven worthwhile.

This might be the message in dealing with the leper. The tongue may be utilized constructively in all aspects that will lead to higher purposes and greater goals and elevation of life. This is indicated in the Midrash: "This shall be the law of the leper ... This is alluded to in what is written, Who is the man that desireth life (Ps. 34:13).

"This may be compared to the case of the peddler who used to go around the towns in the vicinity of Sepphoris, crying out: 'Who wishes to buy the elixir of life?' and drawing great crowds around him. R. Jannai was sitting and expounding in his room and heard him calling out: 'Who desires the elixir of life?' He said to him: 'Come here, and sell me it.' The peddler said: 'Neither you nor people like you require that which I have to sell.' The Rabbi pressed him, and the peddler went up to him and brought out the Book of Psalms and showed him the passage, 'Who is the man that desireth life? What is written immediately thereafter? Keep thy tongue from evil, depart from evil and do good.' R. Jannai said: 'Solomon, too, proclaims. Whoso keepeth his mouth and his tongue keepeth his soul from troubles' (Prov. 21:23). R. Jannai said: All my life have I been reading this passage, but did not know how it was to be explained, until this hawker came and made it clear, viz. 'Who is the man that desireth life ..? Keep thy tongue from evil, etc.' It is for the same reason that Moses addressed a warning to Israel, saying to them, this shall be the law of the mezora (leper) i.e., the law relating to one that gives currency to an evil report (mozi (shem) ra)." (*Midrash, Leviticus* 16:2)

27. Holy—and Human

The Torah deals with the concept of holiness. The text reads: "And the Lord spoke unto Moses, saying: Speak unto all the congregation of the children of Israel and say unto them: Ye shall be holy; for I, the Lord your God, am holy." (Leviticus, 30:1-2)

There are two basic requirements in Jewish tradition for an act to be described as truly holy: One, that it be performed in public, open to view and knowledge. Two, that it be performed on a human level.

In a striking passage we are told that holiness, as well as the sanctification of God, must have a public aspect. The Talmud says: "All things pertaining to holiness should be done only when there are ten or more present." (*Talmud, Berakot,* 21b)

In this connection Moshe Sofer notes that the religious recluse who deprives himself of much of the worldly pleasures and social contacts is much more prevalent among non-Jews than among Jews. Jewish life does not encourage religious separation from other members of the community. One does not have to go into isolation in order to comprehend the works of God by living the life of a hermit. One should rather establish social contacts and associate with people. Through association with others and establishing a healthy interaction with people, one can better understand the greatness of God and thus perfect himself. (Moshe Sofer, *Torat Moshe,* vol. 2, p. 50b)

Common thinking associates holiness with angels and with the supernatural. Jewish tradition, however, emphasizes that we, man, must try to achieve holiness on a human level, one which he reveals in spite of all his mortal frailties.

Acts of holiness must be performed on a human level because Jewish laws and practices are not given to angels but to human beings. Holiness in Jewish life is able to emerge despite man's weaknesses and his lack of strength and endurance. He can perform eloquently and gallantly as a man in matters of holiness. Indeed, man is the more praiseworthy for overcoming his shortcomings. This concept has been alluded to in the Midrash.

Rabbi Abin said "It is like the case of a king who had a cellar full of wine. The king placed watchmen over it, some of them Nazarites (those who must abstain from wine) and some drunkards. At evening time he came to give them their wages, and gave the drunkards two shares and the Nazarites one share. The Nazarites said to him: 'Oh, Lord, the king! Have we not all watched alike? Why do you give these drunkards two shares and us one share?' The king answered them, 'These are drunkards and are accustomed to drink wine, and so I am giving these two shares and you one share.' It is the same with the celestial beings, the Evil Inclination is not existent among them . . . but as for man—the Evil Inclination sways him . . ." (*Midrash Rabbah*, Leviticus 24:8)

Man's activities may be considered holy only when man is man, when he is human and with human limitations and frailties. Religion and holiness which man is able to experience is manifested only in a human expression.

Human beings can lead a saintly existence but only on a human level, with activities that pertain to human beings. And only this is required of man. And because man performs noble human activities he elevates God and becomes holy. As it is suggested in the Midrash: "Because you are elevating Me (says the Lord) by being just so do I rest my holiness among you." (*Midrash Rabbah, Deuteronomy* 5:6)

28. How Good Is Our Leadership?

What is the picture of the emergence of leadership in contemporary Jewish life? Throughout the ages Jews have produced many excellent leaders, not only in areas of Jewish affairs, but also in academic, intellectual and political fields as well. To a great extent they still do. The chief criteria for achieving high position and status in the oft hostile environments was true excellence. However, the criteria for leadership in Jewish community affairs today is not always excellence.

In community affairs, particularly in present-day American Jewish life, leadership seldom emerges from within the confines of the specific endeavor in question. When it does, the criteria for selection is not necessarily superiority on past performance. For example, in the field of education, the leaders are not necessarily those who excel in education, in learning, or scholarship. In the area of religion, the leaders are not necessarily the most pious ones. The leaders of Jewish congregations are seldom elected because of the deep conviction of their faith, observance of rituals, or understanding of Jewish prayers.

On what basis are Jewish leaders selected? In general, they are chosen for their outstanding capacities. However, various other reasons are frequently operative: one, because of ability in areas other than that for which leadership calls; two, because of ability at persuading, impressing, pretending and maneuvering; three, and most unfortunate of all, because of availability when others in the community refuse to serve. In this event one becomes a leader by default, because of lack in manpower resources.

This was not so, traditionally in Jewish life.

We find a helpful lesson on this in this scripture which deals primarily with the prescription of the spiritual and personal life of the *kohanim,* the priests. The text begins: "and the Lord said unto Moses: speak unto the priests, the sons of Aaron and say unto them . . ." (*Leviticus* 21:1-2).

Rashi, quoting the Talmud (*Yebomot* 114a), explains why the text repeats itself with God saying: "speak unto the priests" and "say unto them." The rabbis learn from this that elder priests or those of higher standing were obligated to speak to their juniors concerning the observance of the priestly duties and obligations.

Definite reference is made here about the proper leadership that existed among the priests. There has been a clear distinction among the rank order of the priests. This rank order is clearly classified into explicit offices with specific rank and function. Priests belonging to these categories had special duties, clothing and even their private lives were clearly prescribed by law. Thus, among the *kohanim* there was a clear distinction between the *gedolim,* senior rank, and the *ketanim,* junior rank order.

Furthermore, leadership among the priests was to be achieved within their own rank and order, and within the realm of their own activities. The Talmud states that the high priest who was "the highest among his brethren" (Leviticus 21:10) had to emerge from among his own brethren and had to excel first and foremost his own brethren. (*Talmud, Yuma,* 18a)

In addition to having the ability to surpass his own brethren, the high priest had to excel them in five specific areas: 1) in *wisdom* (he had to show intellectual excellence); 2) in *strength* (he had to possess strength of character and also physical ability); 3) in *beauty* (he had to have pleasant features and a kind appearance); 4) in

71

wealth (although "if he was not already rich, his fellows made him rich") and 5) in *age* (he had to show ability and experience). And at the moment he was anointed with the anointing oil, he became superior to all his brethren. (*Midrash Rabbah, Leviticus,* 26:9)

Jewish leadership, today as in the past, should require higher standards than those which are so prevalent nowadays. Jewish leadership, particularly in Jewish affairs, should require at least JEWISH-NESS as its major prerequisite.

29. Booths—and Slums

True democracy assures the freedom of the individual, as well as, the freedom of the group. Freedom of the individual means that every person in a society has the right to do whatever he wants within the limitations of law.

Freedom of the group means that every group, including members of minorities, in a society, has the right to produce from within its ranks "good," as well as, "bad" members; "conformists," as well as, "non-conformists," "observers," as well as, "deviants."

The deviants and the non-conformists have no reflection upon other members of the group.

The meaning of freedom reaches beyond the confines of social conformity. Only then can there be an ideal democracy in which a minority group can afford the luxury of producing social deviants without identifying and branding the entire group with and because of them.

This also means that persons engaging in socially unacceptable occupations place no reflection or hardship upon the group of which they are members. Social deviation must be an individual matter. The deviant alone should face the consequences of the negative sanctions of society and not the group.

But this type of democracy does not exist in our society, and certainly not in any other societies. To a great extent individuals are identified with the group of which they are members.

Accordingly, we may pose a question: Does a Jew have the moral right to be a slum landlord in America today?

I am cognizant of the many problems these landlords have in connection with their property. I realize that the owner of any slum did not have to import dirt and debris into his property. Most likely, the trash was left in the house from the previous occupant, and additional dirt was brought in by the current occupant.

I further recognize much of the unequal distribution of goods and services based on race in our society. Recent study has shown that about 60 percent of non-whites become school dropouts, whereas for the whites it is only 30 percent. About 5.4 percent of non-white population of young adults between 25 and 29 years of age have completed college, whereas 12 percent of whites of the same age have completed college.

Family income for Negroes has fallen consistently below that of whites by one-third or more. The migration pattern of Negroes from South to North, from rural slum to urban slum makes it difficult for them to break down the wall of poverty and cultural deprivation. (John Walsh, "Advanced Degrees . . ." *Science,* Sept. 13, 1963)

Aside from these facts and beyond the framework of legality, ownership of slums by Jews presents a religious-moral issue.

In the Torah the Jew is told to sit in a booth for seven days on the holiday of Succoth because he should remember that his forefathers sat in the succah.

The text reads, "You shall dwell in booths seven days; all citizens in Israel shall live in booths, in order that generations may know that I made the Israelite people live in booths, when I brought them out of the land of Egypt, I the Lord your God." (Leviticus 23:42-43)

The Jew is commanded on this holiday to build for himself a booth, a temporary cottage, to remind him of the inadequate housing he had when he came out of Egypt. In America too, we build a succah, make a blessing in it, and recall that it was this type of housing in which our forefathers lived after the exodus.

But for the Jew, the succah, representing inadequate housing, is not only a Biblical description; it is not only a theological symbolism associated with the ancient Jew of the Bible.

Not so long ago, inadequate housing for the Jew was a reality. The parents, or the grandparents of today's slum landlords most likely lived in the inadequate housing of Poland, Russia, Galicia, or even in the ghettoes of New York, Chicago and Philadelphia.

To us Jews, the meaning of the holiday of Succoth is not something far removed, something abstract or foreign. Sitting in the succah on this holiday recalls not only the cottages of the desert, but the many inadequate houses in which Jews lived throughout the ages.

We enter the succah on this holiday as a religious performance and thanksgiving, fully aware of the fact that, by grace of God, today the Jew in America can live in elegant homes and desirable neighborhoods.

Hence we are reminded in the Bible, "You shall live in booths seven days . . . in order that future generations may know" and never let our children forget that it was this type of home in which the Lord made the children of Israel dwell. As a contrast, let us be thankful for those homes in which we live and which we own today.

True, in an ideal democracy minority group members have the right to deviate, perhaps in the same proportion as the majority group, provided they are willing to face the consequences as individuals. However, this ideal democracy has not been reached.

In addition, slum landlords do not only invite community censorship and identification with the entire group, but they also challenge Jewish past and traditional values.

People that celebrate such a holiday as Succoth recalling the inadequate housing of their own, have a responsibility to be sensitive to community sentiments which consider it morally wrong to earn a living from inadequate housing of others.

Perhaps community leaders and rabbis may work out a program by which slum landlords may dispose of their property without suffering greater financial loss than is necessary. So that *"you shall keep the holiday of Succoth . . . and shall rejoice in your feast . . . because the Lord your God shall bless you . . . in all the works of your hands . . ."* (Deuteronomy 16:13-15)

30. How Good the Vine

The Jew has been charged so often with having characteristics which are not complimentary. A great deal has been said about his "clannishness," "aggressiveness," "overt religiosity" and "intellectuality," to mention a few. Jews even had a tendency to defend all these "charges" and "accusations" and to point out that these traits are not necessarily characteristic of Jews. Most of the traits are prevalent among all peoples. The problem is not the fact that the traits are associated with the Jew, so much as the fact that the context in which the association is alleged places him in a very derogatory light.

Interestingly enough, these characteristics are not only to be found among Jews, but their emergence and development became essential for the survival and identification for the Jew. This paradox can be understood with the aid of a Midrash.

The Midrash draws a beautiful parallel between the vine and the people of Israel. Every one of these comparisons could be misconstructed and given a negative meaning. However, it enumerates most of the basic characteristics that became functional for the survival of the Jew.

1. CLANNISHNESS: *". . . as the vine is not planted haphazard, but in rows by rows, so are Israel arranged under separate banners by families."* Jews developed a family system which considers the good wife as beyond the price of rubies. It provides sentiments concerning the family from which the awesome and respected *Yiddishe Mammeh* emerged. The strong emotional ties in the Jewish family are among the most binding forces the Jew has.

2. AGGRESSIVENESS: *". . . as the vine is lower than all other trees and yet is predominant among all the trees, so are Israel; they appear as though they are inferior, but in Time to Come they may inherit the world from one end to another."* In a hostile world in which he could call nothing his own, the Jew had to emphasize lofty thoughts, and nourish the hope that he too would inherit a world. And if it was not possible in this world for him to reach out and be free all over the world, then perhaps in the World to Come he could have that opportunity.

3. INTELLECTUAL IMPACT: *". . . as from the vine a single bough comes out and eclipses many trees, so are Israel; one righteous man comes out of them and may have an enormous impact upon the whole world."* Throughout the ages the Jew has produced many great leaders who had an impact upon the development of civilization. The Jew deeply cherished these great names. No matter how far one was removed from the major stream of Jewish life he took pleasure and satisfaction in associating himself with these men of history.

4. RESPECT FOR THE LITERATE AND THE SCHOLAR: *". . . as in the vine the leaves cover the clusters, so it is with Israel; the ignorant among them protects the scholar."* The great admiration for scholars among Jews can be seen even in our days as Jewish

parents show such great concern about the education of their children. Since Talmudic times the Jew took with him the institutions of learning, the *Bet Sefer,* or the *Heder,* on the primary level and the *Bet Hamidrash,* or the *Yeshiva* on the secondary level. It was through the protection and support of non-learned men that scholars were able to continue with their studies.

5. HUMILITY OF THE TRULY GREAT: "*. . . As the vine contains large and small clusters, the larger ones appearing to be lower than its neighbor, so are Israel; whosoever of them that labors in the Torah and is actually greater than his neighbor in Torah, appears lowlier than his neighbor.*" The truly great in Israel were able to attract many followers because of their humility. These leaders were able to reach down and lift up those who needed encouragement and strength. The movement of Hasidism is an excellent example where the master through his own humility was able to lift the ignorant and the unsophisticated.

6. NON-COMPLIMENTARY ELEMENTS: "*. . . as the vine provides wine as well as vinegar, the wine requiring a benediction and the vinegar requiring a benediction, so it is with Israel; they are under the obligation of pronouncing a benediction for that which is good as well as for that which is bad.*" Jews always had among them the sinful, the corrupt and even the depraved. But Judaism provided social institutions and agencies where solutions were sought and adjustments achieved. Seldom, if ever, did Jews rely completely upon sources other than their own institutions. The unfortunate among Jews were always considered part of the community and therefore a responsibility of the community.

7. MOBILITY: "*. . . as in the case of the vine its fruit first is trodden down with the foot and it is set on the table of kings, so are Israel; they appear as if rejected . . . but they become elevated.*" In my lands and at many times the Jew arrived with his wandering staff in his hands and with his pack on his back. Yet if only some opportunity was given, he was able to move upward and lift himself out of his miseries. He aimed for dignity, for liberty and for human elevation.

8. SUPPORTED BY THE TORAH: "*. . . as the vine is propped up by a cane, so is Israel supported by the merit of Torah.*" Ethics and justice derived from the Torah gave the Jew the basis for his value system; the observance of the Torah gives the Jew his Jewish character.

9. CONTINUITY WITH THE PAST: "... *as the vine is propped up by dry stakes and is itself fresh, so Israel relies upon the merit of their forefathers, although these are asleep. Hence it is written* THEN WILL I REMEMBER MY COVENANT WITH JACOB." Although the Jew had many social forces that tied him with his fellow Jews, the major force for Jewish identification is his past. He considers himself a *yichus*, a distinguished birth. He links himself with Jewish history. And by so doing he reenforces Jewish continuity for ever.

IV. From
THE BOOK OF NUMBERS

31. In the Wilderness of Sinai

The fourth book of the Torah in Hebrew is called *Bamidbar*, literally, "in the wilderness," the key word in the opening verse. In English it is called the Book of Numbers because in it is reported the taking of the census on two separate occasions. The first census was taken as the Israelite people were comping in the wilderness of Sinai in the second year of their wandering.

The text reads, "On the first day of the second month, in the second year following the exodus from the land of Egypt, the Lord spoke to Moses in the wilderness of Sinai . . . take a census of the whole Israelite community by the clans of its ancestral houses . . ." (Numbers 1:1-2)

The Midrash comments, why in the wilderness of Sinai? Our sages have inferred from this that the Torah was given to the accompaniment of three things—fire, water and wilderness. *Fire*—whence is this derived? From the text "Now Mount Sinai was enveloped in smoke because the Lord descended upon it in fire." (Exodus 19:18) And *water*—whence is this derived? For it is said, "The heavens also dropped water." (Judges 5:4) And *wilderness*—whence is this derived? From the text "And the Lord spoke unto Moses in the wilderness of Sinai." (*Midrash Rabbah Bamidbar* 1:7)

In every generation the Jew has renewed, with fervor, his determination to continue to study the Torah and to consider it as the major source of guiding principles for his life. As it was in the past so will it be in the future. In order to appreciate the Torah as the basis for Jewish life in our generation, we may profitably consider the significance of the fire, water and wilderness mentioned in the Midrash above.

Fire is associated with self-sacrifice, an essential element of perpetuating Torah in our lives. The Talmud relates: "Rabbi Simeon the Shilonite lectured: 'When the wicked Nebuchadnezzar cast Hananiah (Shadrach) Mishael (Mesheck), and Azariah (Abednego) into the fiery furnace, Yurkami, Prince of hail, rose before the Holy One, blessed be He, and said to Him: 'Sovereign of the Universe! Let me go down and cool the furnace and save the righteous men from the fiery furnace.' Said Gabriel to him, 'The might of the Holy One, blessed be He, is not thus manifested, for thou art the Prince of hail, and all know that water extinguishes fire. But I, the Prince of fire, will go down and cool it within and heat it without and will thus perform a double miracle'." (Talmud *Pesachim* 118 a-b)

For the perpetuation of Torah and for the glorification of God the great men in Israel were always willing to be thrown into fire. The observance of the Torah does not require that one be consumed by fire because the Torah was given to "live in it." However, it is necessary to show spirit, willingness and self sacrifice.

Water is associated with the belief and dependence upon the will of God as it has been said, "As water is essential to the entire world in summer as well as winter so is doing the will of the Creator essential to all beings. Furthermore, as water is the life of all the world, so is the word of the Torah." (*Tanah Debei Eliyahu Rabbah* 18) Certainly for the Jew the Torah became the basis for his identification and the major stream for his continuity.

What about the association with the wilderness and the Torah? One of my Jewish college students wrote once in a term paper that because of the lack of religious education and upbringing in his home, when he came out into the larger world, he found himself in a wilderness. In his wilderness, there were no streets to guide him, there were no trees to shade him, and there were no homes to shelter him. He was all alone. He had no direction to follow. A Jew must become aware that without Torah his religious life is without a sense of direction.

God gave the Torah explicitly in the wilderness, void of all previous tradition. In it existed only the children of Israel and the Torah as their directing guide. The wilderness had no other attractions except the newly developing culture based upon the living words of God. In this wilderness God revealed himself and gave the Jews worth and value, law and guidance.

32. Should One Hate?

The major ingredient of this ancient priestly benediction is peace. The text reads: "And the Lord said unto Moses 'Speak unto Aaron and unto his sons saying: This way shall ye bless the children of Israel; ye shall say unto them: the Lord bless thee and keep thee; the Lord make his face to shine upon thee, and be gracious unto thee; the Lord lift up his countenance upon thee and give thee peace." (Numbers 6:22-26)

The Midrash adds "Peace is great, for even during war peace is necessary . . ."

Great is peace for even the dying need peace . . .

Great is peace for even the angels that dwell on high need peace, as it says: 'He maketh peace in His high places' (Job 25:2) Now an inference can be drawn a *minori ad majus*. If peace is necessary in a place where there is not hatred or enmity, how much more is this the case in a place where all these qualities are found? (*Midrash Rabbah Naso* 11:7)

Comments about war and peace that are made today, usually refer to a possibility and prevention of a third world war. Much of the essays written on the subject deal with warning signals and calling attention to a threat of a nuclear war. The desirability of peace is mentioned to bring to mind the great danger of the possibility of a global annihilation of all human life.

Now and then we do hear a different kind of concern over peace. This concern over peace is not related to a hypothetical future but rather to an actual past. It is not associated with forthcoming hostility but rather with present attitudes. In her recent book, *Eichmann in Jerusalem,* Hannah Arendt contends that Eichmann was misjudged by the world. She expresses astonishment that nobody believed Eichmann when he said, "I myself had no hatred for the Jews." She also considers the trial a failure and charges that the court did not give "a valid definition of the crime against humanity." She further states that similar crimes may be committed in the future and "no punishment has ever possessed enough power of deterrence to prevent the commission of crimes." The question may be asked: Does this mean that it was a mistake to punish Eichmann?

These and similar sentiments may appear proper in a world of peace and rationality. But there are many who did not make peace either with themselves or with their world. Elie Wiesel tells in an article "An Appointment with Hate" that he was asked by a student what he thought Germany was like. He replied, "I imagine it abject and kneeling, filled with ruins and cemeteries, sobbing with fear and remorse. I imagine it famished and tormented, its inhabitants crawling on the ground begging for pardon and oblivion." But instead he finds that the Germans argue, "If we are not judged, it is because we have done nothing. We are innocent. Hitler? The world could and should have stopped him in time. It did not, it must share our guilt. The camps? Their existence was known in Washington, in London, in the Vatican. No voice was raised in protest against Auschwitz. The German people were not the only ones silent . . . Why blame us only?"

Wiesel concludes his article saying: ". . . today even having been deserted by my hate . . . I cry out with all my heart against forgiveness against forgetting against silence. Every Jew, somewhere in his being should set apart a zone of hate—healthy virile hate—for what the German personifies and for what persists in the German. To do otherwise would be a betrayal of the dead." (*Commentary,* Dec. 1962)

There are still many angry people, particularly those who were in the concentration camps, in whose faces death stared. They did not make peace with themselves and certainly not with the world. They are praying to have energy to hate. They hate because they do not want to betray the dead. They have internal war to generate emotional hostility to keep their memory alive.

We cannot ask them to make peace with themselves and with the world . . . But we can ask "May it please the Lord to bless the children of Israel with peace at all times and hours." We must ask for peace because even during internal war peace is necessary; even those who have gone to eternity need peace and if peace is necessary in a place where there is no hatred or enmity how much more do we all need peace.

33. The Elders of Israel

"The Lord said unto Moses 'Gather unto Me seventy men of elders of Israel whom you know to be the elders of the people, and officers over them; and bring them into the tent of meeting, that they stand there with you . . . and they shall bear the burden of the people with you'." (Numbers 11:16-17) Moses, however, was not certain about the criteria for selection. What are these characteristics that qualify one to become an elder in Israel?

In order to understand the qualifications of an elder, we must consider the Midrash. The Midrash explains that "when Pharaoh said: 'Come, let us deal wisely with (the Jews)' . . . and they did set over them task-masters, (Exodus 1:10-11) he gathered together all Israel and said to them: 'I beg of you, work with me today as a personal favor.' The king took a basket and a trowel, and when the Israelites saw Pharaoh carrying a basket and a trowel and working among the bricks, they too went to work with all their might. When dusk fell he appointed taskmasters over them and said to them: 'Reckon up the number of bricks.' Thereupon they rose and counted them. Then Pharaoh said to them: 'This number you must produce each day.'

"Pharaoh appointed Egyptian taskmasters over the officers of Israel, whereas the officers were put in charge of the rest of the people. When Pharaoh said to them: 'You shall no more give the people straw . . . and the tale of the brick . . . you shall lay upon them.' (Ibid. 5:7-8) the taskmasters came and counted the bricks. If they found the number deficient the taskmasters smote the officers; as it says 'And the officers of the children of Israel . . . were beaten.' (Ibid. 5:14) The officers allowed themselves to be smitten for the rest of the people and did not hand them over to the taskmasters thinking: It is better that we should be smitten and that the rest of the people should not be exhausted.

"Consequently, when the Holy One, blessed be He, said: 'Gather unto Me seventy men of the elders of Israel, Moses said to the Holy One: Sovereign of the Universe! I know not who is worthy and who is not.' God said to him: 'whom you know to be the elders of the people, and officers over them,' namely those elders and officers who submitted their bodies to be smitten for the people's sake in Egypt on account of the total of bricks, let them now come forward, and accept of this greatness. For this reason it says, 'whom you know to be the elders of the people, and officers over them.' In return for their having submitted themselves to be smitten for the community, 'they shall bear the burden of the people with you'." (*Midrash Rabbah*, Numbers 15:20)

Thus the criteria for becoming an elder in Israel is selflessness, ability and willingness to provide protection and security for others even through great personal sacrifice.

The ability to provide security and protection to Israel is a consistent qualification in other areas of religious symbolism. Before God gave the Torah, He said to the children of Israel: "You have seen what I did unto the Egyptians and how I bore you on eagles wings . . ." (Exodus 14:5) The Mekilta adds: "Why is the eagle distinguished from all other birds?" (The answer is) all other birds carry their young between their feet, being afraid of other birds flying higher above them. The eagle, however, is afraid only of men who might shoot at him. He, therefore, prefers that the arrows lodge in him rather than in his children.

To give a parable, (the Mekilta continues): "A man was going on the road with his son walking in front of him. If robbers, who might seek to capture the son, come from in front, he takes him from before himself and puts him behind himself. If a wolf comes from behind, he takes his son from behind and puts him in front. If robbers come from in front and wolves from behind, he takes the son and puts him upon his shoulders. (God did the same to the children of Israel) as it is said: And in the wilderness, where thou hast seen how that the Lord your God bore you, as a man bear his son." (*Deuteronomy* 1:31)

As the eagle symbolically, so the elders of Israel factually, brought the children of Israel closer to God. As the eagle, so the elders of Israel must have as their qualification the ability to provide protection and security—a condition under which the Torah will remain in Israel.

34. Riot in the Community

As the children of Israel were camping near the land of Canaan, Moses sent scouts to investigate the country. Moses charged them to go to the South and up into the mountains and see the land, and the people that live in it; whether they are strong or weak, whether they are few or many; and whether the land is good or bad; and whether they live in camps or strongholds; and whether the land is fat or lean; and whether there are trees therein or not.

The scouts came back with samples of Canaan's fruits—pomegranates, figs, and a cluster of grapes that had to be carried by two men. They told the children of Israel that the land is indeed flowing with milk and honey but its inhabitants are fierce, the cities are great and fortified, Amalek lives in the land, all the people are giants and that the Israelites looked like grasshoppers in comparison to them.

Upon hearing this report the congregation of Israel wept all night and murmured against Moses and Aaron and said unto them: "Why did God bring us into this land? Is it to fall by the sword and that our wives and children become a prey? Were it not better for us to return to Egypt?"

Moses and Aaron fell on their faces before the whole congregation of Israel and Joshua and Caleb rent their clothes and said: "If God delights in us He will bring us into this land . . . only rebel not against God." And as a result of this riot God swore that with the exception of Joshua and Caleb none will enter the Promised Land. (*Numbers* 13:1-14, 14:5, 24)

The disturbance in the community, the rebellion of the people, the anger of God and the final punishment was due to the fact that the scouts spread an evil report of the land . . . Their report was not necessarily lies, falsehood and untruth, but rather a distortion of facts. The evil was associated with the manner of their presentation and the circumstances under which they reported. Upon closer examination we can recognize that it was not so much what they said but how they said it and the effect it made on the people. They utilized practically all those methods that are most effective for rabble rousing and riot stimulation.

1. *Time*

After a long journey in the desert the children of Israel built up strong expectations of coming into the Promised Land, flowing with milk and honey. After the years of slavery they expected to enter a land which was ready and waiting for their coming. Now the scouts came and gave the "wrong" information, during the peak of the people's expectations. The Israelites should have been prepared for the news. But instead they were told at a most inappropriate time, enough reason to stir them to riot.

2. *Discouragement*

Israel was full of enthusiasm, hoping to go into the Promised Land without any trouble. After all, they crossed the sea with little difficulty because God was leading the way. Thus they were expecting news that would reaffirm their own belief and enthusiasm. Man usually wants to hear that which he already believes. But the scouts came back creating the impression that the people have to fight giants and fortified cities. This discouragement was enough reason to stir people to riot.

3. *Association with fear and hatred*

The first enemy the children of Israel met after their exodus from Egypt was Amalek. The Jews were attacked in the back and still had a very bad taste in their mouth from the battle. Now the scouts came back and mentioned first Amalek with whom they already had a very unpleasant experience. The psychological association of the Promised Land and Amalek was enough reason to stir the people to riot.

4. *Making comparisons*

The scouts did not only give a pure fact-finding report on Canaan but they expressed an opinion as well. They made comparisons between the Israelites and the inhabitants of the land. They said that the Israelites looked like grasshoppers in comparison to them—enough reason to stir anyone to riot.

5. *Sensationalism*

The scouts' report was not geared to give a factual report on their findings but they designed their report so as to produce a startling effect on the listeners. Their purpose was to excite and arouse feelings and to create false impressions.

6. *Exaggeration*

The scouts magnified their statement beyond the limits of truth. They overstated and presented their findings disproportionately to the facts—stirring to riot.

Throughout the ages history has taught us that thrilling impressionists, sensationalists, those who discourage and belittle can always stir individuals to riot and mob behavior. Looking into the various aspects of the many unfortunate intergroup relations today we could easily discover that some of these methods are very effectively used. Stirring people and stimulating them to irrational actions always had unfortunate consequences. Why don't we learn a lesson from the scouts of Israel?

35. Serving with Integrity

The leadership of Moses, the greatest rabbi in Israel, was challenged. Korah, one of the outstanding Levites, a cousin of Moses and Aaron, felt that he had not been given proper honor and opportunity for leadership. He went to the tribe of Reuben, associated himself with Dathan and Abiram, who since their early days in Egypt had been trouble makers, and they rose up against Moses. Korah, Dathan and Abiram and 250 eminent men gathered against Moses and Aaron and said to them: "You take too much upon you! All the congregation are holy; everyone of them (equally heard the commandments of Sinai from God). Why then, do you lift up yourself above the assembly of the Lord? (If you Moses have taken the kingship, you should not have selected your brother Aaron to the priesthood!)" (*Numbers,* 16:3)

When Moses heard the public charges he fell upon his face and said unto them: "In the morning the Lord will make known who is His, and who is holy (and worthy to serve him as priest). This is what you should do, (the 250 of you) take censers . . . and put fire therein and put incense upon them before the Lord . . . and the man whom the Lord chooses, he shall be holy." (*Ibid.* 16:5-7)

Meanwhile Moses sent for Dathan and Abiram to conciliate them with peaceful words, but they said that they are not coming. "Even if you send to put out our eyes, if we shall not come up to you, we shall not come." (*Ibid.* Rashi 16:14)

Moses was angry and said unto God "respect not their offering, not one ass have I taken from them, neither have I hurt one of them." (*Ibid.* 16:15)

The Midrash adds, Moses said "Even that which I had the right to take I did not take from them. Normally if a man works for the sanctuary he receives his wages from the sanctuary. In my case, however, when I went down from Midian to Egypt and had a right to take from them an ass, seeing that I was going on their business, I did not take one. Furthermore, I did not condemn the innocent nor acquit the guilty." (*Midrash Rabbah,* Numbers 18:10)

It is interesting to note that Moses who could have enumerated many other virtues and personal characteristics about his selfless service to Israel singled out this one aspect that he was just and had not taken anything from Israel even when it was coming to him. Obviously this must convey to us a great moral teaching.

In a public office the most important prerequisite is having clean hands. The acquisition of gain by dishonest, unfair means through the abuse of one's position or office is denounced in any civilized society. Thus, to refuse bribe or "graft" is not a remarkable virtue. About bribe the Torah warned ". . . the Lord of Lords, the great God, the mighty and the aweful, regarded not the person that takes bribe." (Deuteronomy 10:17) Also it is written about judges and officers: "You should not respect persons; neither shall you take a gift, for a gift blinds the eyes of the wise, and perverts the words of the righteous." (*Ibid.* 16:19)

But Moses' great virtue was that he did not take anything from the Jews for his services, even when it was coming to him.

Oh, how great and admirable a public servant can be if his actions and decisions and public deliberations are above and beyond any reproach, any accusation. Oh, how high can one hold his head if his judgments and determinations are not influenced, nor can they be claimed to be influenced by pecuniary considerations.

We must be cognizant of the fact, however, that in modern society, with its complex system of division of labor it would be impossible for public servants to be aloof from material considerations. Nonetheless, the rare privilege of those men whose leadership depends only on their own conscience and the high standards of their call is most enviable.

36. "Hear Now, You Rebels!"

After Miriam died, the children of Israel had no water to drink. They assembled before Moses and Aaron and quarreled, saying: "It would have been better for us to perish by plague, the way our brethren perished, rather than to die of thirst. Why did you bring us out from Egypt into an evil place like this?"

Moses went into the tent of the meeting and fell upon his face. And the Lord spoke to him saying: "Take the rod, and gather the congregation . . . and speak to the rock before their eyes . . . and you shall bring forth water from the rock . . ."

Moses took the rod and gathered the congregation and said unto them: "Hear now you rebels! Out of this rock are we to bring forth water for you?"

And Moses lifted up his hand and struck the rock twice with his rod and water came. And God said unto Moses and unto Aaron: "Because you did not believe in Me to sanctify Me before the children of Israel, therefore you shall not bring this congregation into the land which I will give them." (*Numbers* 20:1-12)

Maimonides (Rambam) and Nachmanides (Ramban) hold diverse views regarding the reasons for Moses' punishment. Maimonides states that Moses was punished because he was angry and insulted the children of Israel by saying: "Hear now, you rebels! . . ." Nachmanides states that Moses was punished because he struck the rock instead of speaking to it.

Both viewpoints can be well supported. Nachmanides is upheld by the text which specifically states that God said to speak to the rock, but instead Moses struck it. Maimonides' view is supported by a statement of the Midrash: "Because they (Moses and Aaron) said 'Hear now, you rebels' they were punished for their speech—'therefore you shall not bring this assembly into the land which I have given them'." (*Midrash Rabbah, Genesis* 99:5)

However, both viewpoints represent basically one concept. Namely, Moses was punished because in his anger he insulted the Jews. To understand this more fully, we may consider a Hasidic thought. It has been told that Rabbi Israel Bal Shem Tov, the founder of Hasidism, strongly objected to the visiting preachers who scolded the Jews in their preaching. He maintained that, *Auf Yiden redt men nisht kan shlechts*, one does not speak evil of a Jew.

The story is related that once such a preacher came into the community and spoke harshly about the sins of Israel. Upon his conclusion, the Bal Shem Tov reprimanded him for publicly insulting his brethren. The preacher defended himself saying: "We found in various places in the Torah that Jews are chastised for their sins."

"It is true," said the Bal Shem Tov, "God is often angry with us and punishes us, but this prerogative is never given to a human being. Even Moses who was the greatest leader of the Jews was punished when he said to them: 'Hear now, you rebels!' Because for this he was not allowed to enter into the promised land."

It seems that the two viewpoints, expressing the reason for Moses' punishment is basically one, namely, *insulting the children of Israel*. Speaking harshly and striking the rock was practically the same mode of behavior, moved by anger. Moses in his anger spoke harshly and struck the rock, thereby sublimating an action which he perhaps intended for the children of Israel.

May this serve as a lesson to those who so frequently find faults with some of the actions of their brethren. May we all learn not to be quick with words or with the rod when there is a question about the condemnation of Israel.

37. 'Curse or Blessing'

The Bible describes in full detail the blessing of Balaam. Although his utterances are among the most beautiful passages of the Torah, the rabbis consider them to be derogatory implications.

As Rashi said: "From the blessings of that wicked (Balaam) we may learn that curse was in his heart." (Rashi, *Numbers* 24:6) Even the beautiful passage uttered by Balaam which the Jew recites upon entering the synagogue, "How fair are your tents O Jacob, your dwellings O Israel!" is an indication of curse, according to the rabbis.

When Simon Sofer arrived in Cracow, Poland, to fill the position as chief rabbi, he found about 100 *minyonim* and *stiblach*, small houses and synagogues where permanent worship services were held. As was the custom, wherever 10 Jews gathered, they established a *minyen*, a permanent worship service.

In his inaugural speech, Rabbi Sofer commented on this problem saying: "Masters, since I came to this community I have a clear understanding of Balaam's blessing, 'How fair are your tents, O Jacob, your dwellings O Israel.' Balaam, as you know, did not have a great desire to bless the children of Israel. He only did so by deistical force and compulsion. But when he was shown that among Jews there are many 'worship tents' and many different houses of study, he was delighted. He called out in a loud and happy voice, 'How fair are your tents O Jacob . . .' implying that he is glad to see Jews divided into many places of worship.

"Balaam understood that this synagogal division is more of a curse than a blessing. In fact, Balaam hoped that the Jews would create many more divisions among themselves by having separate synagogues and separate houses of worship.

"Divided synagogues would only make the differences among

Jews that much greater, and the separation among them that much more pronounced. This sort of blessing still remains with the Jews to this very day, as you can see in Cracow.

"This division," continued Rabbi Sofer, "has been an old pattern among Jews since ancient times. The Talmud says: 'It has been taught, Rabbi Judah stated . . . that in the Alexandrian synagogue in Egypt the seating was not socially integrated; the goldsmiths sat separately, the silversmiths separately, the blacksmiths separately, and the weavers separately so that when a poor man entered the place he recognized the members of his craft and went to them . . .' (*Talmud Sukah* 51b)

"Thus, every occupational group has chosen a specific corner in that synagogue, the same way as it is today; a *minyen* of tailors, a *minyen* of shoemakers, etc., all separated from other groups." (*Kelilat Joffe*)

I doubt whether in contemporary American Jewish communities the synagogues are divided by an occupational order as in Cracow or in Alexandria, but it is unquestionably true that a definite division does exist. This division is not necessarily based on denominational affiliation and intense religious behavior, but rather on a very loosely defined stratified order of social class.

Although in America today occupation is an important stratifier, social economic levels are of greater significance. Thus much of synagogue affiliation today is based on social levels. People join those synagogues with whose members they would like to affiliate socially.

The only question is, what is the basis for stratification? Whereas in Alexandria and in Cracow it was the type of occupation, in American Jewish communities it is the *level* of occupation, or the *prestige* associated with the occupation. An individual who does not rank as high as others in the Jewish community aspires to a social rank similar to that of the members of a synagogue. He is hopeful that through social mobility he will reach a position that will enable him to associate freely with those who occupy the seat of envy in his eye.

It is difficult to believe that this system of stratification in synagogue affiliation strengthens Jewish life. However, future generations will be the judge as to whether this was a curse or a blessing.

38. Replacing a Moses

Man builds many hopes and expectations during his life, many of which remain unfulfilled when he has to leave this world. Because of the uncertainty of time, man seldom prepares himself for his departure. Knowing that one has to leave while his plans are still un-implemented and unaccomplished is one of life's most unpleasant feelings.

Not only individuals of no consequence leave without putting their house in order. Public leaders of great consequence are also among those who do not allow replacement during their life time. As a result, many organizations go down with their leaders—the once great institution sinks or disintegrates holding the memory of its past glory and the sign of its leaders' inadequacy and selfishness.

In many communities even after a leader died he was not replaced for years, because no one was considered his equal in wisdom and scholarship. Although often this was an expression of honor to the great man, nonetheless the community suffered because it did not extend the opportunity to a younger man to develop the office and himself through his personal growth and accomplishment.

This pattern is not in line with Biblical practices. Jewish life considers no one indispensable, even Moses, the great leader of Israel was replaced. The episode is described. Before he died, Moses said to God: "Let the Lord set a man over the congregation who shall go out before them, who shall come in before them, who shall lead them out, and who shall bring them in; and the congregation of the Lord be not as sheep without a shepherd."

The Lord said: "Take Joshua, the son of Nun and lay your hand upon him; and set him before Eleazar the priest, and before all the congregation, and give him a charge in their sight. And you shall put of your honor upon him, that all the congregation of the children of Israel may listen." (*Numbers* 27-16-20)

Thus, we are told that the leader *is* replaceable and that he *must* be replaced in his life time. In addition to these conditions, upon closer observation we can notice that the Torah describes the necessary qualifications, and the procedure of the appointment of the new leader.

Qualifications of the Leader:

1. *"A man over the congregation . . ."* The leader should be a

94

man among men; a man, a human being, not an angel, one whose thoughts and life patterns are not removed from human emotions and frailties (Rabbi Menahem Mandel from Kotzk). He should be a man, possessing the qualities of a man, the ability of dealing with human problems on the level of man. Furthermore, he should be a man *over the congregation* and not the congregation over him.

2. "*. . . who shall go out before them . . .*" The leader should act not in the manner of those kings who sit in their homes and send forth their armies or representatives. He should act as Moshe who fought against Sihon and Og himself (Rashi, *Numbers* 27:17). The fight for community perpetuity and solidarity should be headed by the leader, he should go before the congregation and show them the way.

3. "*. . . who shall come in before them . . .*" The leader should be the first one to come into the tent of Torah to study and perform. He should not only preach but become also an active participant. Let him show leadership through his own exemplified activities.

4. "*. . . who shall bring them out . . .*" The leader should not only come out with new ideas but he should be able to bring out the best in the congregation.

5. "*. . . who shall bring them in . . .*" The leader should be able to bring the congregation back should they have moved too far. Also the leader should be able to bring himself back if he has advanced too far from that which was necessarily in the best interest of the congregation. He should be flexible depending upon the religious needs, emotional stability and background of the individual constituents.

Procedure of the Appointment of the Leader:

In addition to the leader's qualifications, we also learn something about his procedure of appointment. The way the new leader is appointed is clearly described in the Torah. The following are the steps taken:

1. "*. . . Take for you . . .*" Take a person who is acceptable to you. The candidate should be acceptable to the old retiring leader. It may be his protege, as in the case of Joshua.

2. "*. . . a man in whom is spirit . . .*" The new leader should be a man with spirit and enthusiasm, forthright and with fortitude.

3. "*. . . and lay your hand upon him . . .*" He should be a man who has matured and developed under the guiding hands of the old leader.

4. *". . . and set him before Eleazar the priest . . ."* The new leader must be acceptable to the existing religious authorities.

5. *". . . and before all the congregation . . ."* The leader must be acceptable to the entire congregation.

6. *". . . and charge him in the presence of the congregation . . ."* The old leader should have no private dealings with the new one. There should be no private or secret deals made of which the community is not aware.

7. *". . . and you put your honor upon him . . ."* Once the new leader is appointed the old leader should give his support, honor and respect, and not divide the congregation by enacting double loyalties.

Should Jewish communities adopt these attitudes and procedures and should the leaders acquire highly qualifying characteristics, the Jewish world could look forward to a wholesome, cohesive community life and leadership.

39. Mixed Motives

The Torah relates the event of a successful war the Israelites waged against the Midianites. It tells how Israel seized as booty Midian's beasts, herds and wealth.

When Israel reached the Jordan River, the children of Reuben and Gad came with a request before Moses, Elezar the priest, and the chieftains of the community. They argued that since they owned much cattle, it should not be demanded of them to cross the Jordan, but that they should be allowed to stay in the land which had just been conquered.

Moses suspected that the motive behind this request was the fear of battle. Thus he asked: "Shall your brothers go to war while you stay here?" The children of Reuben and Gad came forward and explained that while they wished to build sheepfolds for their flocks and towns for their children they were nevertheless willing to continue fighting. They promised that they would not return to their homes until every one of the Israelites would be in possession of his portion of land.

Furthermore, they promised that they would not claim any share with the rest of the Israelites on the other side of the Jordan. Moses replied that if they would continue fighting until the end of the war, until the land would be conquered, "then they shall be clear before the Lord and Israel." (*Numbers* 32:1-23)

Although according to the text the children of Reuben and Gad seem to have acted properly, the rabbis looked upon them with disdain. The Midrash includes them with persons of whom the rabbis speak derogatorily. Our Rabbis taught: Two wise men arose in this world, one in Israel and one among non-Jews; Ahitophal[1] in Israel and Balaam[2] among the nations of the world—and both of them were destroyed from the world.

Similarly, two strong men arose in the world, one in Israel and one among the nations of the world—Samson[3] in Israel and Goliath[4] among the nations of the world—and both of them were destroyed from the world.

So, also, two rich men rose in the world, one in Israel and one among the nations of the world—Korah[5] in Israel and Haman[6] among the nations of the world—and both of them were destroyed from the world. Why? Because their gift was not from God, but they snatched it for themselves.

Likewise in the case of the children of Reuben and Gad, you find that they were rich, possessing large numbers of cattle, but they loved their money and settled outside the land of Israel. Consequently they were the first of all the tribes to go into exile . . . What brought

---

[1] Ahitophal was the privy councillor of David who showed himself devoid of moral principle by his participation in the rebellion of Absolom (II *Samuel* 15:12; 17:21-23)

[2] Balaam the son of Beor was a prophet of Pathor in Mesopotamia. When he saw that he could not curse the children of Israel, he advised Balak to tempt the Jews to immoral acts (*Talmud Sanhedrin* 106a). He was killed by the sword (*Numbers* 31:8).

[3] Samson was a judge in Israel. The rabbis say that his eyes were put out because he followed them too often (*Talmud Sotah* 9b)

[4] Goliath the Philistine giant of Gath was slain by David (I *Samuel* 17:4). In addition to being of uncertain paternity (*Midrash Ruth* 1:14), he stood with arrogance before God (*Talmud Sotah* 42b). He challenged the Israelites every morning and evening to disturb them while they were reciting the Shema (*Yalkut* 2:126).

[5] Korah the son of Izhar rebelled against the leadership of Moses and Aaron (*Numbers* 16:1-3). According to the rabbis he incited the people against Moses arguing that it was impossible to endure the laws instituted by Moses (*Midrash Rabbah Numbers* 18:2-3).

[6] Haman the Agagite, the chief minister of King Ahasuerus (*Esther* 3:1-2), built gallows for Mordecai and went to the house of study where he found Mordecai surrounded by many students all with ashes on their heads, clad in sackcloth . . . It was the cry of these children that brought doom on him (*Midrash Rabbah Esther* 9).

97

it on them? The fact that they separated themselves from their brothers because of their possessions. (*Midrash Rabbah Exodus* 22:7).

Despite the fact that the settlement of the children of Reuben and Gad outside Israel was approved by Moses, their act was nevertheless unfavorably viewed. First, their motives were questioned. Moses thought that they were "draft dodgers," afraid of the war, who did not want to continue fighting with the rest of the children of Israel.

Furthermore, they expressed selfishness by wanting to settle before their brothers. In addition, even after they declared their willingness to continue in battle, the justification they gave for settling themselves early was to build sheepfolds for their flocks—a cause that hardly reflects high moral standards. It is for these reasons that they are compared with individuals whose moral standards were also questionable.

Hence, before engaging in activities in which one's motives may be questioned, let purity of purpose be manifested. Let the activities reveal innocence, freedom from any moral wrong. This is what Moses said to the children of Reuben and Gad that they must be cleared of having evil motives in their planned activities.

In addition, Moses indicated that if they wished to stay on this side of the Jordan, at least they should have reversed the order of importance of the factors listed.

The children of Reuben and Gad asked permission to provide folds for their sheep and towns for their children. But Moses reversed the order indicating that it would be much more appropriate to build cities for the little ones, and thus plan for the future generation and only after that to build folds for their sheep.

If we could come clean before God and men, plan for a future world, and take care of our possessions, in this order of importance, we too might look forward with greater optimism to the generations ahead.

V. From
THE BOOK OF DEUTERONOMY

40. The Chastisers and the Chastised

The fifth book of the Torah in Hebrew is called "Devarim," literally "words," the key term in the opening verse. The book is also known as "Mishnah Torah" because much of what has been said previously is repeated in it. In English it is called "Deuteronomy" after the Vulgate, Latin version of the Scriptures.

The text opens: "These are the words that Moses addressed to all Israel, on the other side of the Jordan—through the wilderness, in the Arabah, near Suph, between Paran and Tophel, Laban, Haze-roth, and Di-zahab." (*Deuteronomy* 1:1)

Rashi quotes the Sifre explaining that these addresses of Moses were in the main devoted to reprimanding and reproving the children of Israel for improper behavior which had provoked the ire of God. The roster of geographic locations—difficult to understand if taken literally—was of places in which the provocations against God had taken place.

In every society man develops values and standards by which he compares and approves, or disapproves other people's behavior. Usually he considers his own superior to others.

We, too, have developed certain standards and consider our society the most civilized yet and one that is associated with high moral values. Therefore we, too, have the tendency to sneer and to sniff at the behavior of the past generations, particularly those of our forefathers as related in the Bible.

However, the question may be asked: Would we have acted differently if we would have participated in the 40 years wandering of our forefathers? Or, better, yet, do we act differently today in similar circumstances?

Let us briefly review the events for which the Jews were reprimanded:

In the wilderness the provocation of Israel was associated with their grave concern for food. As it is related in the Torah: "In the wilderness, the whole Israelite community grumbled against Moses and Aaron. The Israelites said to them: 'If only we had died by the hand of the Lord in the land of Egypt, when we sat by the fleshpots,

101

when we ate our fill of bread! For you have brought us out into this wilderness to starve this whole congregation to death'." (*Exodus* 16:2-3)

In Arabah the provocation of Israel was in connection with their licentious behavior. As the Torah relates: "While Israel was staying in Shittim (Arbot Moab) the people profaned themselves . . . with the Moabite women . . ." (*Numbers* 25:1-2)

At Suph the provocation of Israel was in connection with their fear of Pharaoh. As the Torah relates: "As Pharaoh drew near, the Israelites caught sight of the Egyptians advancing upon them. Greatly frightened, the Israelites cried out to the Lord. And they said unto Moses, 'Was it for want of graves in Egypt that you brought us to die in the wilderness? What have you done to us, taking us out of Egypt?' " (*Exodus* 14:10-11)

Between Paran and Tophel the provocation of Israel was in connection with their dissatisfaction of the manna. As the Torah relates: ". . . and the people spoke against God and against Moses, 'Why did you make us leave Egypt to die in the wilderness? There is no bread and no water, and we have come to loathe this miserable food'." (*Numbers* 21:5)

In Hazeroth the provocation of Israel was in connection with rebellion against authority—Korah's against Moses and Aaron. As the Torah relates: "(Korah and his associates) gathered against Moses and Aaron and said to them, 'You have gone too far for all the community are holy . . . Why then do you rise yourself above the Lord's congregation?' " (*Numbers* 16:3)

In Di-zahab the provocation of Israel was in connection with the making of the "golden calf." As the Torah relates: ". . . the people gathered against Aaron and said to him, 'Come, make a god who shall go before us, for that man Moses, who brought us from the land of Egypt—we cannot tell what has happened to him.' . . ." (*Exodus* 32:1)

In these geographic locations the children of Israel provoked God, for which they were reprimanded by Moses. Considering the temperament of the American Jewish community, we may ask: Would our behavior under similar conditions and circumstances be superior to those of our forefathers? How would we react to our leaders' scolding and censure? Furthermore, who are the individuals who qualify to reprove and to reprimand today?

It seems that the rabbis were much concerned with these questions. The Talmud relates, "It was taught Rabbi Tarfon said, 'I wonder whether there is anyone in this generation who accepts reproof? Because should one say to another "Remove the mote from between your teeth" (indicating he has done wrong) the other would answer, "Remove the beam between your eyes," (indicating that the reprover has done wrong even of greater consequence).

"Rabbi Eleazar ben Azariah said, 'I wonder if there is anyone in this generation who (is qualified or) knows how to reprove.' Rabbi Jochanan ben Nuri said, 'I call heaven and earth to witness for myself that often was Rabbi Akiba punished through me because I used to complain against him before our Rabban Gamaliel and all the more he (Rabbi Akiba) loved me for it, (indicating that there are still those who accept reproof, and that there are qualified reprovers)." (*Talmud Arakin* 16b)

Perhaps we can reach a higher plane by realizing how much of our personal and communal behavior patterns need reproof, how easily susceptible we are to the total roster of temptations. At the same time we sadly recognize the lack of truly qualified reprovers.

41. The Pain of Aging

Aging is a great problem in our society. While science contributes to man's longevity, while social systems provide more and more for his economic security, very little is being done for his psychological adjustment to old age.

Man grows old bereft of significant social status, waiting for a hopeless tomorrow. We can easily imagine the pain that cuts so deeply when a man recognizes that yesterday he was the symbol of power and today he is merely groping in utter helplessness.

Yesterday he was in command of his world and today he is seeking the sympathies of others. Yesterday he made this world for himself and today this world is no longer his own.

The comments of the rabbis on the Scripture clearly indicate the great psychological problem of aging as it is portrayed by the aging leader Moses. The text reads: "And (Moses) besought the Lord at that time saying, 'O Lord God . . . let me go over, I pray You, and see the good land that is beyond the Jordan . . .' But the Lord was angry with me . . . and said . . . 'speak no more unto Me of this matter . . . for you shall not go over this Jordan. But charge Joshua, and encourage him . . . for he shall go over before this people and he shall cause them to inherit the land' . . ." (*Deuteronomy* 3:23-28)

Recognizing the many problems of aging and the kind of psychological pain and agony that are associated with it, the rabbis brought to our attention three major considerations as they are related to Moses, the leader of Israel:

1. Change in Status
2. Exclusion from the Life of the Community
3. Introspection and Soul Searching

Change in Status—the leader during his time in office establishes a very high status rank and enjoys the prestige that is associated with his office. Sometimes he and the office he occupies become synonymous in the eyes of the members of the community. Nevertheless, when his hour is past, and he retires from the office his status becomes that of a private citizen.

Thus, "Rabbi Abin said, (the circumstance that Moses had to beg God for a special privilege) can be compared to a king who had a favorite, who had the power to appoint generals, governors, and commanders-in-chief. Later the people saw him begging the gatekeeper to let him enter the palace, and he would not permit him. Everyone was amazed at this and said, 'Yesterday he was appointing generals, governors, and commanders-in-chief and now he vainly begs the gate-keeper to let him enter the palace.'

"The answer given to them was, 'His hour is past!' So, too, with Moses, once whatever he ordered God would fulfill . . . and now he begs and prostrates himself to be permitted to enter the land of Israel, and his prayers are not accepted. His hour is past . . ." (*Midrash Rabbah Deuteronomy* 2:3)

Exclusion from the Life of the Community—In addition to the recognition of the passing of time which is inevitable, the rabbis recognized the psychological agony of the great man as he realizes that he is being excluded from the life of the community. He finds out that his life's work and his contributions were for the sake of others and he himself is not included in all he has done.

Thus, the Sifre states, "(When Moses was refused permission to enter the land of Israel, he) said to the Lord, 'You opened up the opportunity for me to pray for your children and I stood before You and prayed for them and You heard my prayers and forgave their sins. And all these times I thought that I too, and my personal requests were also included in my prayers' . . ." (*Sifre Debarim* 3:24)

Introspection and Soul Searching—In addition to his change of status and his gradual exclusion from community life, the great man conducts a *Chesbon hanefesh*—a soul searching exploration of his own conscience. He wants to make certain that he has served adequately and that he did not corrupt his high office or call. He wants the assurance that his retirement is not a sign of God's punitive measures for doing wrong in an official capacity.

The leader wants to know that, if he has done wrong, he has erred in his individual capacity, on an individual basis but not by corrupting his office, or corrupting others through his office. Moses wanted that it be known that his sin was a personal one, and not in line with his duty in instructing the Jews of the Torah.

Thus, the Midrash relates, "Moses said before God, 'Master of the Universe, let my sin be written down for future generations!' Rabbi Samuel said, 'This may be compared to a king who issued a decree that whoever should gather and eat from the fruits of the Sabbatical year (which was prohibited) should be made to walk around the public assembly grounds. One woman went and gathered and ate of the fruits; and she was made to walk around the public assembly grounds. She said to the king, 'Your Majesty! I implore you, let these fruits be suspended from my neck so that the people of the city shall not say that I am guilty of witchcraft or some act of immorality; and when they see the fruits around my neck they will know that it is on their account that I am made to walk around the public assembly grounds!'

"So Moses said before God, 'Let my sin be written down for future generations that Israel may not say, Moses falsified something in the Torah, or he spoke something which he had not been commanded (and for that he was punished by not being permitted to enter the land of Israel); and they shall know that it was merely because of the water (a personal matter where I did not fully obey the words of God).'" (*Midrash Rabbah Deuteronomy* 2:6)

42. Recognizing Human Values

The Jew has been warned in the Torah to turn to God. He is told ". . . If you search . . . for the Lord your God, you will find Him, if only you seek Him with all your soul . . ." (*Deuteronomy* 4:29)

Prophet Hosea's call is more emphatic as he says, "Return O Israel, unto the Lord your God for you have stumbled in your iniquity. Take with you words and return unto the Lord . . ." (*Hosea* 14:2-3).

According to Jewish tradition, it is within the power of every man to redeem himself by repenting. Repentance is an earnest resolution to break away from sin and turning to God. As Prophet Isaiah warned, "Let the wicked forsake his way, and the man of iniquity his thoughts; and let him return unto the Lord and He will have compassion upon him . . . for He will abundantly pardon." (*Isaiah* 55:6-7)

And because "there is not a righteous man upon earth, that does good, and sinneth not . . ." (*Ecclesiastes* 7:20) it is the duty of every Jew to repent.

Jewish law distinguishes between offenses committed against God and offenses against man. The law prescribes that if one sinned against God ". . . he shall confess wherein he has sinned and he shall bring as penalty to the Lord, for the sin of which he is guilty . . . a sacrifice . . ." (*Leviticus* 5:5-6). In addition, he shall make a solemn promise and a firm resolution that he will not commit the same sin again. (*Talmud Yuma* 87b and Maimonides, *Yad*, Teshubah)

However, if one has sinned against man, then, in addition to confession and sacrifice, he shall make a restitution in full of whatever has been wrongly obtained. If the wronged man has died, restitution shall be made to his heirs. (*Ibid*).

But what about the offenses we have committed against our fellow men where restitution cannot be made? After all, offenses we commit against our fellow men in a civilized society are not necessarily robbing them, cheating them or doing them bodily harm. The offenses we commit against our neighbors may be reaching deeply into their very soul of being.

Perhaps we may ask ourselves some of these questions: How often have we judged other men by the first impression they made

106

on us? How often did these external impressions place people into categories of "good" and "bad"? How often did we classify people into categories of "worthy" or "unworthy" of our kindness and personal friendship and other pertinent considerations? How often did we offend our brother because of sheer carelessness or tactlessness?

A beautiful story is told about the great Rabbi Shneur Zalman of Ladi, the originator of the Lubavitcher dynasty. The rabbi used to show exceptional kindness and personal attention to insignificant, unassuming, and simple people. The rabbi went out of his way to accord these people much respect and honor.

On one occasion, a wealthy diamond dealer, the rabbi's follower and admirer, had enough courage to ask: "Rabbi, why do you pay so much respect and honor to simple, unsophisticated, unlearned and undistinguished men?" The rabbi remained silent and did not say a word.

Some time had passed when the wealthy diamond dealer visited the rabbi again. At this occasion he displayed before the rabbi some of the most beautiful precious stones that were in his possession. About one stone in particular the dealer remarked, "This is the most beautiful stone I have ever seen in my entire experience. There are not many stones like this in the entire world. It is the most perfect gem of its kind."

"I do not see anything extraordinary in this stone," remarked the rabbi in a casual tone of voice. "This stone looks to me just like the others. I do not understand why you have such an exceptional praise for this one."

"I am sorry, rabbi," said the dealer in embarrassment. "One must know diamonds in order to appreciate the value of this stone. One must be an expert to understand the fine lines, the exceptional brilliance, the purity and the perfection of the cut of this stone."

"Don't you think that the same applies to human beings?" said the rabbi earnestly. "Don't you think that one must know the inner self of human beings before passing judgment over them? Don't you think that one must be an expert on human qualities before we can evaluate our fellowmen?"

In a society where secondary social relationship is the rule, many individuals fail to perceive or recognize human values and admirable characteristics in others. Perhaps by according more respect, honor, and personal recognition to one's friends, neighbors and associates, one could even become an expert of human qualities.

43. Judges and Justice

One of the pillars upon which the social world is based is justice. The administration of justice is one of the greatest virtues conceivable to man. Without justice there could be no law, no order and no society. Giving to everyone what is his due; conducting human relationships through honesty, integrity, and fairness; having an equal distribution of right, is the basis of every human society.

Whenever human misery came upon societies, wherever pain and suffering was inflicted upon the peoples of the earth, it was mainly because justice, fairness, propriety, and impartiality had been gravely violated by man. Thus the administration of justice has been so important in Jewish life that the Talmud declares: "Every judge who judges with complete fairness even for a single hour, the Scripture gives him credit as though he had become a partner to God in the creation of the world." (*Talmud Sabbath* 10a)

Injustice is not always based on malicious design. Injustice, on the contrary, could be based upon *kindness*. We try to be kinder to one person than to another in the administration of justice. We are willing to overlook failure and deficiencies with one and not with another. We tend to have double standards one of which we apply to ourselves and one to others.

This deals with appointing judges in Israel. The text reads: "Appoint judges and officers for yourselves for your tribes in all the settlements which the Lord your God is giving you, and they shall judge the people with due justice.

"You shall not judge unfairly; you shall show no partiality; you shall not take bribes, for bribes blind the eyes of the wise and pervert the words of the righteous. Justice, justice shall you pursue that you may live and inherit the land which the Lord your God is giving you." (*Deuteronomy* 16:18-20)

The biblical conception of justice, *sedek,* is basically righteousness. It is not abstract or formal theological principle, but has its basis in the conception of the community as grounded in a covenant relation between God and man, and man and man. It is primarily an inward quality, the presupposition of right action, which makes healthful, wholesome and harmonious personal community life possible. (Vergilius Ferm, *An Encyclopedia of Religion*, p. 663)

Justice is the most important phenomenon in maintaining a cohesive community life. Unlike charity, benevolence and love, which are voluntary obligations, justice is an involuntary obligation with definite and universal connotation of rights and privileges of others in society. Justice has played such an important role in Jewish life, the election of judges occupies an essential position in community organization. Let us observe some of the comments of the rabbis on the text dealing with the appointment of judges.

Appoint judges and officers . . . which the Lord your God is giving you . . . Appoint such judges who are able to bring godliness into the community . . . (*Botzino Danhura*)

. . . They shall judge the people . . . only after they have thoroughly judged themselves; only after they have met all those standards which they are going to apply to others . . . (*Keli Yakor*)

Appoint judges . . . in all the settlements . . . There should be an abundance of judges. They should be available in all cities and towns. (*Talmud Sanhedrin* 16)

Appoint judges . . . for yourselves . . . The judges must judge even those who elected them into office. Thus a rabbi who is appointed the spiritual leader of the congregation should have the authority even over those who elected him into office. (*Hatam Sofer*)

Appoint judges . . . for yourselves . . . but not for other nations. (*Midrash Rabbah*) Sometimes there is the tendency to appoint an individual into office in order to make a good impression on others. But the main criteria for an appointment should be the ability to fulfill the needs of the community first and foremost. (*Naftali Sofer*)

Appoint judges . . . for your tribes . . . "Rabbi Semeon ben Gamaael says, 'each tribe must judge its own members . . .'" (*Talmud,* op. cit.) because the norms of the community are best understood by its own members. (It should be noted that judges who are members of a specific ethnic group are assigned to judge a member of his group, even in our society. However, the thought is shattering as one questions the administration of justice in those cases.)

You shall show no partiality . . . There should be no favoritism shown to the wealthy or the poor. The judge should not be lenient even toward the unfortunate, because this too, is injustice. (*Sifre*)

You shall not take bribes . . . Not only should a judge take no bribes for acquitting the guilty and condemning the innocent, but he should take no bribe for even acquitting the innocent and condemning the guilty. (*Ibid.*)

A people that has experienced so much injustice as the Jew, must appreciate the value of justice. Injustice among those who have been victims of injustice is surely inexcusable. The very existence of the Jew and his behavior should be the personification of justice.

This idea was so strongly stressed by the rabbis that the Talmud states Rabbi Jose ben Elisha said, "If you see a generation overwhelmed by many troubles go forth and examine the judges of Israel, for all retribution that comes to the world comes only on account of the judges of Israel." (*Talmud Sabbath* 139a)

Justice can exist in a society that values justice. Only that society can value justice whose members will internalize integrity and fairness into its social norms. Internalizing fairness and integrity, on the other hand, will always depend on the individual.

The Talmud states, "The Holy One, blessed be He, will not cause His Divine Presence to rest upon Israel until the wicked judges cease out of Israel." (*Ibid.*)

44. "The Rebellious Son"

The Torah gives us a detailed description of the "Rebellious Son." The text reads: "If a man has a disloyal and defiant son, that does not heed his father or mother, and does not obey them even after they discipline him, his father and mother shall take hold of him and bring him out to the elders of his town at the public place of his community. They shall say to the elders of his town, 'this son of ours is disloyal and defiant; he does not heed us. He is a wastrel and a drunkard.' Thereupon the men of his town shall stone him to death. Thus you will sweep out evil from your midst; all Israel will hear and be afraid." (*Deuteronomy* 21:18-21)

This passage is very difficult to comprehend. Were there really children under age of 13 who were so incorrigible that the only solution was for them to die? Were there really parents who took their children to the elders of the city and let them be stoned because they were disobedient?

What about the community? Were the people of the community ready and anxious to come out and stone a child because he was defiant and disloyal to his parents? How about the parents? What was the parents' responsibility? What happened from the birth of the child until the moment they decided to take the child to be stoned?

Furthermore, who were the parents? What was their position in the community? What about the legal and moral rights of parents disposing of children as individual human beings? How can this procedure be reconciled in a civilized society? Did organized social systems ever take life that casually that for parental disobedience children could be stoned?

In all probability the actual occurrence of the rebellious son has never taken place. First, the legal technicality as prescribed by the rabbis was so complex that to become a "rebellious son" was practically impossible. The rebellious son could not be of legal age as he no longer was under the jurisdiction of his parents. He could not be under legal age as he was not fully responsible for his irreligious behavior.

Thus he had to be 13 years and a day old and show signs of physical maturity. Second, his crime had to be of a peculiar nature. He had to steal money from his father and buy with it meat and Italian wine and eat and drink in a degrading manner. (*Mishnah Sanhedrin* and Maimonides. *Mishnah Torah,* Hilchot Mamrim, ch. 7)

The additional legal technicalities necessary for one to be considered a "rebellious son" were so complex that all the necessary variables were never present. Hence according to the Talmud "it never happened and it will never happen . . ." (*Talmud Sanhedrin* 71a).

Despite the fact that there was little or no likelihood for a "rebellious son" to take place in Israel, nevertheless, its lesson, its teachings convey a message of great importance and significance.

The Talmud relates an interesting argument between Rabbi Simeon and Rabbi Jonathan regarding the rebellious son. "Rabbi Simeon said: 'Just because one eats a *tartemar* (weight) of meat and drinks a half a log of Italian wine shall his father and mother have him stoned? Thus, it never happened and it will never happen.' . . . Rabbi Jonathan said, 'I saw him (the rebellious son who was executed through his parents) and I sat on his grave'. . . ." (*Ibid.*)

The two rabbis represent two different viewpoints. Rabbi Simeon places the emphasis upon the parents. Thus he argues that it is hardly probable for parents to have their child stoned for committing a misdemeanor. Rabbi Jonathan, on the other hand, places the emphasis upon the child. He is concerned that parents may have their child legally stoned as a punitive measure for his behavior.

He feels that the parents have already executed their child long before they brought the matter to the attention of the authorities. In fact Rabbi Jonathan indicated that the occurrence of such a rebellious child is not only possible but that he himself has witnessed one, and, in his great sorrow, sat on one's grave.

In order that the message of the rebellious son may be even more meaningful I shall briefly review some aspects of crime and juvenile delinquency in our society today.

It should be noted that the more highly civilized a society becomes the more it tends to associate crime with the larger social order and less and less with the individual's responsibility for the behavior of their children.

Today we speak about (1) *the cost of crime*. It has been estimated that the annual cost of crime in the United States is about $13 billion.

In addition to the economic considerations of crime, we hear that "juvenile delinquency is (2) *the by-product of generations lost in the confusion* and bewilderment of the uprooting." (Joseph P. Fitzpatrick, "The Puerto Rican," *Catholic Mind*, May-June 1960)

We are further told (3) that juvenile gangs belong to a *subculture* that has its own standards and values which are different from those that prevail in the normative society. (Albert A. Kohn, *Delinquent Boys*, Glencoe: The Free Press 1955)

Or we are given to believe (4) that juvenile crime is the result of the eternal *intergenerational struggle* between the young and the old. (Herbert Block. "The Juvenile Gang: A Cultural Reflex," *The Annals*, May 1963) (5) Even *affluency* has been associated with juvenile delinquency. According to an interesting assertion an affluent society reduces status symbols of class difference to meaningless proportions and consequently society fails to provide adult identification—the child thinks he is an adult and the adult behaves like a juvenile. (T. R. Fyvel, *Trouble Makers: Rebellious Youth in Our Affluent Society*, New York: Schocken Books, 1961)

But we hear very little about the individual's responsibility to social living. We are made aware of society's powerful motivational sources leading to delinquency, but we seldom hear about how much parents themselves contribute to their children's delinquency. We are made aware of the youthful struggle for self-expression of power but we seldom pay attention to the brute facts of familial deprivation and harsh realities of parental inadequacies.

The fact must be recognized that in a developed society the community, through its various arms and agencies assumes more and more of the responsibility that once was within province of the family. But as these responsibilities are assumed by the city, state and Federal governments, parents should not obliviate themselves from the parental duties of child-rearing which basically must be their, and their only, primary responsibility.

Thus our text is not necessarily concerned with the punitive measures of the child but rather with the responsibility of the parents. The text can be understood as follows: *If a man has a disloyal and defiant son, who does not heed his father or mother and does not obey them even after they disciplined him* . . . it is about time for them to recognize that the form of discipline is not an appropriate one, and that they are not adequately performing their duties as parents.

His father and mother should take a hold of him . . . but not someone else. They ought to know their child! They should be able to answer to what happened to him all those years.

How did he become disloyal and defiant? Did they provide an adequate family life with an atmosphere of warmth, understanding, love, and loyalty? *And bring him to the elders of his town at the public place of his community* . . . with shame and remorse, and admit their parental failure and their lack of responsibility.

They shall say to the elders of his town (admit and recognize) *this son of ours* is the product of our behavior, of our values and conduct, and therefore, no wonder that he . . . *is disloyal and defiant and he does not heed us.* In their shame they should declare *he is a wastrel and a drunkard!*

Now the parents will expect the community to do something, perhaps to correct their failure and mistake. They will expect that the community should rehabilitate a child that has been wronged so often. They should not expect that from the community.

The only thing the community will do is: *Thereupon the men of his town shall stone him to death.* The community will censure him and brand him as a juvenile delinquent, so that he will never have a chance to rise again and become a productive man of society. And although they may think that *thus you will sweep out evil from our midst . . .* but actually, *all Israel will hear and be afraid.*

45. To Remember or to Blot Out?

Remember what Amalek did unto thee by the way as ye came forth out of Egypt; how he met thee by the way, and smote the hindmost of thee, all that were enfeebled in thy rear, when thou wast faint and weary; and he feared not God. Therefore it shall be, when the Lord thy God hath given thee rest from all thine enemies round about, in the land which the Lord thy God giveth thee for an inheritance to possess it, that thou shalt blot out the remembrance of Amalek from under heaven; thou shalt not forget. (Deuteronomy 25:17-19)

To understand why the above passage is read, in a special ceremony, on the Saturday which precedes Purim, it is helpful to remember that Amalek is considered the first enemy and foe of Israel after they had come out from Egypt as a free nation. In the Talmud Amalek stands for Rome and for Edom and Esau from whom they were descended. Amalek, it is noted, inherited Esau's hostility toward his brother Jacob. Thus, he is referred to as "a robber who waylaid Israel," or a "leech eager for blood."

Haman the Agagite who planned a cruel plot against the Jews in Persia, in the days of Ahasuerus, is also associated with Amalek because Haman was a descendant of Amalek.

There is another dimension to the above passage. Although it is recognized by all that Amalek was the arch enemy of the Jew, according to some interpretations, he only performed a divine mission, that of punishing the Jews. Thus it is written:

Then came Amalek and fought with Israel in *Rephidim* . . . Rephidim means *Rifyon-Yodaim* 'feebleness of hands'. Because (Israel) relaxed their hold on the words of the Torah the enemy came upon them. (Mekilta de-Rabbi Ishmael, Amalek)

Against this background we can ask the tantalizing question: *To remember or to blot out?*

The Jew has been commanded to remember his enemy. He was told not to forget! At the same time he was also commanded to "blot out the remembrance" of his enemy. These opposing commandments are somewhat puzzling. What should the Jew do? Should he tell his children "Do not forget that your forefathers met with enemies, like Amalek, Haman and Hitler," and by so doing revive the concept of the eternal suffering of the Jew? Or, should he blot out the remembrance of Amalek and guard and protect his children from the harsh historic facts of the many catastrophes which fill the pages of the Jewish past?

This has been one of the Jewish perplexities throughout the years. Generations came and generations went. Enemies emerged which conquered or were defeated, but most of the time they conquered and left a tragic dent upon Jewish life. After the noise, the storm, the chaos and the holocaust were over, seemingly a stillness pervaded, and the Jew again was facing the same problem: To remember or to blot out? Should one carry on the feeling of antagonism, the hostility, the fear, or blot out the unpleasantness from memory and look forward to a new life—a life which has no relation to the past because "it cannot happen here . . ." and nothing will resemble any of those inhuman activities of a different, uncivilized age . . .

In order to present a further understanding of the implications of this problem, it is helpful to consider the functional significance of remembering or blotting out the memory of the enemy.

Two of the major sociological phenomena that provide strong group solidarity are: 1) external forces; and 2) internal identification. External forces are those social processes which are threatening to the group, like recognizing a fear of a common enemy. Once these exist the group tends to solidify. Internal identification results when members of the group develop common values, attitudes, and behavioral patterns by which they create unifying relationships and common ties.

Actually both factors have helped to solidify the Jew throughout the ages. When the enemy came, the Jew did not ask the question whose Amalek it was. It was recognized as the common enemy; it required group cohesiveness. There resulted the demand to remember the Amalek. And if the Jews had nothing else, they had an Amalek in common. The Jew had to remember because the social circumstances made him recall . . . He could not forget because the conditions of his hostile world did not let him forget . . .

Although remembering the enemy functionally contributed to Jewish continuity, this was a very painful and a negative way to

115

maintain solidarity. There could have been another factor involved in the social process of group solidarity. The maintenance of group cohesion could have been through blotting out the remembrance of the enemy and concentrating on common, living values which the group shares and cultivates. The internal identifying factors of Jews could have become so strong that solidarity should not have depended on the common enemy, or the external threat, but rather on the internal strength, the common values.

Perhaps this positive aspect of group identification is indicated in the story of Amalek. The text reads:

> Then came Amalek and fought with Israel . . . (and Moses stood) on the top of the hill with the rod of God in (his) hand . . . And it came to pass when Moses held up his hand, that Israel prevailed; and when he let down his hand, Amalek prevailed. (Exodus 17:8-11)

To this the Mekilta adds:

> Now how could Moses' hand make Israel victorious or how could his hand break Amalek? It merely means this: When Moses raised his hands toward heaven, Israel would look at him and believe in Him who commanded Moses to do so; then God would perform for them miracles and mighty deeds . . . Rabbi Eliazar says . . . when Moses raised his hands toward heaven, it meant that Israel would be strong in the words of the Torah, to be given through Moses' hands. And when he lowered his hands, it meant that Israel would lower their zeal for the words of the Torah to be given through his hands. (Mekilta, *Ibid.*)

Should positive factors become the predominant solidifiers of Jewish group life, only then will the Jews blot out the remembrance of the enemy and will not need Amalek to remind them . . .

46. Life in Suburbia

Suburbia is relatively a new phenomenon. Some consider it a new type of life, whereas others consider it an additional distance from work. Actually it is an extension of the city, but basically it is designed to provide the conveniences of the city and the comfort of the country.

Much has been written and more has been said about the great evils of the city. Charges were made that in cities people do not establish proper roots because everyone is "on the go." City life brings about an urge for adventure. People do not know and do not care who lives next door.

The cities, the charge continues, are too noisy, too crowded, and too dirty. Working conditions in various factories are not conducive to good health and longevity. People there are said to be unfriendly, aloof, casual, too reserved, too superficial and not always trustworthy. The "moral tone" also, is said to be low and commercialized. (Lincoln Steffens, *The Shame of the City*.)

Furthermore, it has been charged that the institutions of urbanization have taken away many of the functions which formerly belonged to the family. For example, schools have taken over education; policemen have taken over protection; synagogues have taken over religious instruction; waiters and restaurants have taken over feeding, etc. (Carl C. Zimmerman, "The Family," in Joseph S. Roucek (ed.) *Contemporary Sociology*, 1958, p. 92.)

On the other hand, the country has been praised highly. Life there is considered calm; the air is fresh; and the people have a friendlier and closer relationship with one another. Social life is intimate and the familial values are stressed.

However, there is much to be said about the advantages of the city. Everything that is related to expansion and further development emerged in the city. Any progress that civilization may claim is closely related to the development of cities.

Even Judaism first formulated among primitive pastoral tribes in land-locked hills, expanded and developed in cities and adapted to the cosmopolitan, commercial life of scattered people.

Thus, despite the many indictments of urban life, there are many advantages which greatly enhance urban living. Cities provide better water and food inspection, better sanitary conditions, better schools for children, better recreational facilities.

Cities have become research, educational and art centers. Cities provide specialized medical and hospital facilities. The diversified and effective functions of all social institutions are due to development of urban centers.

God blessed the children of Israel saying: *"All these blessings shall come upon you and take effect, if you will but heed the word of the Lord your God: Blessed shall you be in the city and blessed shall you be in the country."* (*Deuteronomy* 28:2-3)

Thus, as the Jew recognizes the advantages of both, the city and

117

the country, he hopes that only the advantages that are associated with the city and the advantages that are associated with the country will come upon Israel as a blessing. (*Hatam Sofer*)

However, according to some rabbis, this passage conveys more than just the blessing of urban and rural living. The Midrash relates Rabbi Yitzchak saying, *"Blessed shall ye be in the city,* on account of the *mitzvot,* good deeds you perform in the city . . . *Blessed shall you be in the country,* on account of the *mitzvot,* good deeds you perform in the country . . ."* (*Midrash Rabbah, Deuteronomy* 7:15)

There are many Jews who are "religious"—observe the traditional Jewish practices only in their homes, but on the "outside" they are afraid that they may be charged with being "old fashioned," or "fanatic," or even a "hypocrite." Thus in the open, in the city, away from home they refrain from free exercise of their religion with pride and dignity.

Thus the Midrash reminds them, *"Blessed shall you be in the city,* on account of all those *mitzvot* you are freely performing in the city, meaning that blessing will come if one will perform adequately in the *city*—in the open, in the market place, before people and among friends." (*Dibrei Shaarei Hayim*)

On the other hand, there are many Jews who exercise all their religious behavior only in the city, only before people, perhaps only in the synagogue, before the public eye. They think that everyone must know their "great" religious deeds. But in their home they are not imbued with religious convictions, do not abide by religious principles.

Thus the Midrash reminds them, *Blessed shall you be in the country,* on account of the *mitzvot* you perform in the country, meaning that blessing will come if one will perform adequately in his intimate environment, in his home, with his family, and in the privacy of his own conscience.

It is not city living or country living per se, that determines one's religiosity; it is the type of life one leads, the kind of values one holds and the activities he performs, in the city as well as the country, that will be the criteria of his religious commitments.

We may move to new suburban developments in order to enjoy the advantages of the city and the country, but let us also take with us the great fervor and educational facilities cities represent and the private and intimate familial values that are represented by country living.

118

47. "Not with You Alone"

Moses assembled the whole congregation of Israel, the heads of the tribes, the elders and the officers, the wives, the children and the strangers, from the woodchoppers to the waterdrawers.

All were standing before God and Moses addressed them, saying: "You stand this day, all of you, before the Lord your God . . . to enter into the covenant of the Lord your God which the Lord your God is concluding with you this day with its sanctions; to the end that He may establish you this day as His people and be your God, as He promised you and as He swore to your fathers Abraham, Isaac, and Jacob.

"I make this covenant . . . not with you alone, but both with those who are standing here with us this day before the Lord our God and with those who are not with us here this day." (*Deuteronomy* 29:9-14)

In every generation in moments of awe, every Jew prepares himself to stand before God. The elders, the officers, the wives, the children, all enter into temples and synagogues and stand before God to reaffirm their covenant with Him. As in the past, so does the Jew today assume the responsibility for himself and for those who will follow after him, to carry on his beautiful tradition.

The Jew confirms his strong faith by declaring that this Judaism, that this Jewish life, with all its meaning and complexities, with all its pains and pleasures, he will further and cultivate. He pledges to sustain, to persist and to preserve this form of life that gave meaning to his existence through so many generations.

Today, as in the past, the Jew is called upon to choose life, to choose that form of life which will keep him together as a people. The life of the Jew as peoplehood depends wholly upon the values and the meanings he attributes to his heritage, to his tradition and to his Torah.

As God said to the children of Israel, "I call heaven and earth witness against you this day: I have put before you life and death, blessing and curse—choose life that you and your offspring may live."

Rashi adds, "The Holy One, blessed be He, said to Israel, 'Look upon the heavens which I created to serve you. Have they ever changed their way? Has the sphere of the sun ever failed to rise in the East? . . . Look upon the earth which I created to serve you. Has it ever changed its ways? Have you ever sown it with seed and

119

it did not sprout? . . . Would it not be proper that you do not change to evil way but choose life?' " (Rashi *Deuteronomy* 30:19)

The Jew is reminded to pursue the unbroken ties of his tradition as the heavens and the earth have continued to follow their natural order. In fact, the Midrash relates that God was pleading with Israel not to forsake His Torah.

"It is compared to a king who had a precious stone which he had placed for safe custody with his friend, saying to him, 'I ask you, take great care of this stone and guard it well; for if it is lost, you cannot afford to pay for it, nor have I another like it. And then you will have sinned against me and against yourself. Therefore, do your duty by both of us and guard it well!' " (*Midrash Rabbah, Deuteronomy* 8:5)

Today too the plea is made to the Jew of the current generation and the generation that will follow, to guard well this great tradition, this noble heritage. In the words of the Midrash, God has given the Jews a precious stone—this Torah, this Jewish life, which until this day has shown the light to the world.

It has given the Jew a specific character. It has taught the Jew to swim in stormy waters of time. It has provided the Jew with the power to survive. It has saved the Jew from social annihilation and assimilation. It has provided the significant link in the chain that connects him to past and future.

Also, God cannot replace the Torah as He declared, "I have not another like it." There is no other Torah. Jewish life is continual. It emerges and develops. It expands and adjusts. But *it is* basically the same.

As Moses said to Israel, "Do not say, 'Another Moses will arise and bring us another Torah from heaven.' I, therefore, warn you. *It is not in heaven* . . . that is to say, no part of it remained in heaven." (*Ibid.* 8:6)

Furthermore, "*It is not in heaven, that you should say, 'Who among us can go up to heaven and bring it for us.' . . . Neither is it beyond the sea that you should say, 'Who among us can cross to the other side of the sea and get it for us.' . . . No, the Torah is very close to you, in your mouth and in your heart to observe it.*" (*Deuteronomy* 30:11-14)

The Torah is part of the Jew's values and judgments and actions. It brings him to reunite with his past. It melts him into a peoplehood and helps him recognize that not with him alone did God make a covenant but with those who came before him and those that follow.

Index

121

Sodom 10
Sofer, Rabbi Moshe 38, 69
Sofer, Rabbi Simen 92, 93
Solomon 27, 68
Soviet Union 7
Steffens, Lincoln 117
stiblach 92
Suburbia 116
Succoth 44, 73, 74
super-ego 4

T

tabernacle 53, 63
Talmid hacham 64
Talmud 8, 12, 24, 27, 35, 40, 43, 48,
    54, 71, 76, 93, 103, 108, 110
Talmudic literature 67, 69
Tamar 27
Tanhum B. Hanilai 66
Taphel 101, 102
Tarfon, Rabbi 103
temple 27, 42, 119
temple service 53
temple ritual 63
Ten Commandments 48, 50
Tetragrammaton 36
Thomas, W. I. 65
Thompson, C. 19
Thompson, Edgar T. 50
Tirard, H. M. 24
Tishri 42, 43
Torah 3, 16, 28, 30, 33, 34, 48-50,
    55, 59, 63-67, 69, 73, 74, 81, 82,
    86, 90, 92, 94-96, 102, 105, 106,
    110

Torat Kohanim 64
Tower of Babel 5

U

United Nations 7
universe 3
Universal Spirit 48, 51-55, 59, 63,
    66, 69-74, 81, 83, 86
Ur 12

V

values 4
value judgment 10
Vayikra 63
Vulgate 3, 33, 101

W

Walsh, John 73
Weber, Max 10, 40
Wiesel, Elie 84
witchcraft 35
world to come 66, 75
worship 16

Y

Yahrzeit 56
Yeshiva 76
Yeushson, B. 68
Yinger, J. Milton 50
Yiskor 56
Yitzchok, Rabbi 118
Yom Kippur 44

Z

Zein, Shlomo Joseph 39
Zimmerman, Carl C. 117
Zipporah 33
Znaniecki, Florian 65
Zohar 20, 21